SHORTHAND
PITMAN NEW ERA

Shorthand is a valuable asset to everyone, whether young or old, in private or professional life. Here, in twenty-five lessons, are presented the rules of shorthand, side by side with exercises, facility drills and dictation tests, so that the reader can practise while he or she learns. Compiled by the experts at Pitman's, this authoritative book is indispensable to anyone—not only secretaries—seeking a first or refresher course in New Era shorthand.

TEACH YOURSELF BOOKS

*Also published in the
Teach Yourself series:*

SHORTHAND
PITMAN NEW ERA

Pitmans College

TEACH YOURSELF BOOKS
Hodder and Stoughton

First published in this format 1983
Sixth impression 1988

Copyright © 1983
Pitman Books Ltd

ISBN 0 340 32436 8

Printed and bound in Great Britain for
Hodder and Stoughton Educational,
a division of Hodder and Stoughton Ltd,
Mill Road, Dunton Green, Sevenoaks, Kent,
by Hazell Watson & Viney Limited
Member of BPCC plc
Aylesbury, Bucks, England
Available in the USA from:
Random House, Inc.,
201 East 50th Street, New York, NY 10022

CONTENTS

INTRODUCTION

It is more than one hundred and forty years since Isaac Pitman invented his famous system of shorthand. Its invention brought with it wonderful opportunities for self-advancement, and the ability to write shorthand has been one of the stepping-stones to success for many a famous person. Its usefulness in all walks of life is so self-evident as not to be questioned, and a knowledge of shorthand is an asset of great value to everyone, whether young or old, whether in private, commercial, or professional life.

There are many who realize this but who do not wish to attend classes. It is to assist such people that these twenty-five Lessons have been prepared. The Lessons are simple and straightforward, and abundant exercise material has been provided. In addition, Facility Drills and Dictation Tests are included so that the learner may acquire considerable facility in writing shorthand outlines side by side with a knowledge of the rules of the system.

Shorthand can be written as fast as speech can be uttered or thoughts expressed in grammatical sequence. Longhand cannot. While longhand is seldom written at speeds exceeding forty words a minute, many thousands of shorthand writers reach speeds of 140 and 150 words a minute, while the system has been written at speeds of 250 words a minute and over. How is this greatly increased speed of shorthand possible? The reason is simple: Pitmans Shorthand is a 'phonetic' system. In longhand writing all the letters of the spelling must be written out: in shorthand writing only the sounds of the word are represented. To represent the simple word *weigh* in longhand, for instance, it is necessary to write five letters, each consisting of more than one stroke. In shorthand it is necessary to represent only the two sounds of the word—the consonant *w* and the vowel sound *ā*, thus: ⌇ The addition of *t*, to make the word *weight* adds several more strokes in longhand writing, but in shorthand the sign is actually reduced to ⌇, the consonant *w* being made shorter to add the sound of *t*. It requires very little study to realize that such signs as ⌇ and ⌇ are written very much more rapidly than the words *weigh* and *weight*.

Because Pitmans Shorthand is written according to the sounds of words and not according to longhand spelling, it is sometimes called *Phonography*, a word derived from two Greek words and meaning *sound writing*. It is particularly important, therefore, for the beginner to pay special attention to the notes regarding writing by sound that are given in the early Lessons of this book.

The presence of *r* in the spelling of a word has a modifying effect upon a preceding vowel in the short-hand outline. Attention is, therefore, directed to the following observations with regard to the consonant *r*, to certain vowels when preceding *r* and to a class of vowels which may be described as more or less obscure.

With the exception of *worsted* (the woollen material) and a few proper names, as *Worcester*, wherever the consonant *r* occurs in a word, in Pitman's Shorthand it must be *represented as a consonant*.

In words such as *bar, far, mar, tar, jar*, the vowel-sign for *ah* is to be used; but in words such as *barrow, marry* and *carry*, the first vowel-sound is to be represented by the vowel-sign for *ă*.

In words such as *four, fore, roar, lore, wore, shore, door, pour, core, gore, tore, sore*, the vowel-sign for *ō* is to be used.

In words such as *torch, morn, fork*, the vowel-sign for *ŏ* is to be used.

In words such as *air*, *fair*, *lair*, *bare*, the vowel-sign for $\bar{a}$ is to be used.

In pairs of words such as *fir*, *fur*; *earth*, *worth*; *per*, *purr*; *Percy*, *pursy*; the vowel-sound in the first word of the pairs is to be represented by the vowel-sign for $\breve{e}$; the vowel-sound in the second word of the pairs is to be represented by the vowel-sign for $\breve{u}$.

In words such as *custody*, *custom*, *baron*, *felony*, *colour*, *factory*, the second vowel-sound is represented by the vowel-sign for $\breve{u}$.

In words such as *village*, *cottage*, *breakage*, the second vowel-sound is represented by the vowel-sign for $\breve{e}$.

In words such as *suppose*, the second vowel-sound is represented by the vowel-sign for $\bar{o}$; but in words such as *supposition*, *disposition*, the second vowel-sound is represented by the vowel-sign for $\breve{u}$.

It is necessary when learning any subject on one's own to be conscientious, for there is no teacher to scold or to praise. Success depends entirely upon one's own efforts. It is advisable, therefore, to set oneself a definite aim. In the case of these twenty-five Lessons, the learner might decide to learn two Lessons a week, thus completing the book in three months. If time did not permit of this, however, the aim might be to learn one Lesson each week. If the learner has plenty of time, he might learn a Lesson a day. The important point is to set oneself a goal, and then to do one's honest best to reach it.

The compilers wish to place on record their acknowledgment of the help rendered in the preparation of this volume by Miss Emily D. Smith, only Holder of the National Union of Teachers' Certificate for shorthand speed writing at 250 words a minute.

LESSON ONE

Shorthand Outlines

As you know, words are made up of consonants and vowels. The outlines of Pitmans Shorthand are also made up of consonants and vowels. The outline for the word *pay* is ⟍, made up of a stroke for the consonant sound *p* and a dot for the vowel sound *ae*. The outline for the word *paid* is ⟍, made up of the stroke for *p*, a stroke for the consonant sound *d*, and the dot for *ae*.

For two further examples, let us take the outline for *toe* ⊢, and the outline for *boat* ⟍. In the first outline there is a stroke for the consonant sound *t* and a dash for the vowel sound *oe*; in the second there is a stroke for the consonant sound *b*, a stroke for *t*, and the dash for *oe*.

Writing by Sound

Look for a minute or two at the four outlines: ⟍ ⟍ ⊢ ⟍. From them you will observe one very important fact about shorthand writing, namely, that in the Pitman system outlines are written *by sound* and not according to longhand spelling. In the two words *pay* and *paid* the longhand spelling of the vowel sound *ae* differs, but in the shorthand outlines this vowel sound is represented in one way only—by the dot. Similarly, the longhand spelling of the vowel sound *oe* differs in *toe* and *boat*, but in the shorthand outlines this sound is represented in one way only—by the dash.

So, write your shorthand by sound. This point is of fundamental importance.

Vowels

There are twelve vowel signs in Pitmans Shorthand, and you have already learned two of them, the dot for the long vowel sound *ae* and a dash for the long vowel sound *oe*. These two signs are placed close to a consonant stroke in the middle position, as in: ⟍ *pay* and ⊢ *toe.*

Consonants

There are twenty-six stroke consonants, and six of these (three very light and three slightly heavier) are shown in the following table. They are all written DOWNWARDS.

Sign	Letter	Name	As in the outlines
⟍	p	pee	⟍ pay, ⟍ paid
⟍	b	bee	⟍ bay, ⟍ bait
l	t	tee	⊢ toe, ⟍ boat
l	d	dee	l· day, l· date
╱	ch	chay	⟩ poach
╱	j	jay	╱ age, ⟩ page

Memorize the six consonants and read the outlines several times, taking careful note of the fact that they are all written by sound. Notice that in the outline for *page* the stroke ╱.... *jay* is used for the second consonant sound, and that although there is a final *e* in the long-hand spelling, there is no vowel at the end of the shorthand outline because the vowel is not sounded. You must write only what you hear when a word is pronounced.

Now take your shorthand notebook and copy the outlines shown above, writing them several times and using a pen with a fine nib. Write very lightly; do not dig into the paper. Where there are two strokes in the outline, the first should rest on the line and the second should be joined to it without lifting the pen. The vowel sign is written in afterwards, thus: ⟍ *pd*, ⟍ *paid*.

PRACTICE ONE (Key on p. 130)
Read and copy several times

(*a*)

(*b*)

Vowels Before and After Strokes

When the vowel sound occurs before the consonant sound, write the vowel sign in front of the stroke; when it occurs after the consonant sound, write the vowel sign after the stroke. Compare the outlines:

⟋ *age*, ⟋ *jay*, ⟍ *ape*, ⟍ *pay*, ⌐ *oat*, ⌐ *toe*, ⎮ *aid*, ⎮ *day*.

Circle S

Among the most common consonant sounds in the English language are the sounds of *s* and *z*. A little circle added to a stroke is used to represent these consonants, as in the outlines: ⟍ *soap*, ⟍ *base*, ⟍ *obeys*, ⎮ *stay*, ⎮ *stays*, ⟍ *spade*, ⟍ *spades*, ⟋ *chose*, ⟋ *sage*.

4

PRACTICE TWO (Key on p. 130)

Read and copy several times

(a) ＼ ＼｡ ｜· ｜· ／· ／· ┐· ┐· ·／

(b) ｜· ｜· ＼ ＼ ＼ ＼ ＼ ＼｡ ＼

Short Forms

Just as the common sounds of *s* and *z* are given a specially brief sign, so certain common words are given specially short signs so that they may be written very rapidly. The words *the* and *a* are extremely common words, for instance, and they are represented by a dot, as: ⋮ *a* (or *an*), ⋯ *the*. All Short Forms should be practised until they can be used without hesitation. Copy the following signs many times—

⋮ *a/an*, ⋯ *the*, ＼ *of*, ＼ *to*, ｜ *it*, ＼ *be*, ＼ *to be*, ⌒ *is/his*.

Phrases

Another device for speeding up writing is to join certain outlines together, writing them without a lift of the pen. It is important that the resulting "phrase" should be easily written and quite clear. Examples of good phrases are: ┕ *it is*, ┐ *of it*, ┐ *to it*, ┐· *to-day*, ⌒ *of his*, ⌒ *to his*, ⌒ *is to*.

You will notice that when two Short Forms are joined together, the first Short Form must be written in its correct position. Compare ┐ *of it* and ┐ *to it*.

As with all Short Forms, phrases should be practised thoroughly.

PRACTICE THREE (Key on p. 130)

Read and copy several times

Note. A small cross represents the full-stop, and two dashes under an outline indicate an initial capital letter, as: *Joe.*

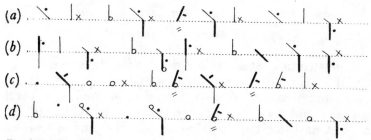

Facility Drill

Daily facility practice will help you to write easily and quickly. Copy out the following drills, leaving three or four blank lines after each line of writing. Using the blank lines, copy from your own shorthand. Make your outlines about the same size as the shorthand in these pages, and write the outlines in the positions shown. There is no need to show vowels after the first two or three copyings.

FACILITY DRILL ONE

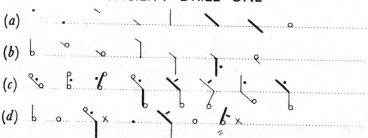

Can you write these 30 outlines (representing 38 words) in one minute?

LESSON TWO

Vowel Signs for Ĕ and Ŭ

You will see from a study of the following six outlines that two new vowel signs are used: $\vert$ *debt,* $\vert$ *Ted,* $\vert$ *jet,* $\diagdown$ *up,* $\vert$ *touch,* $\vert$ *judge.*

The two new signs are a light dot for the vowel sound *ĕ* and a light dash for the vowel sound *ŭ*. You now know two pairs of vowel signs—a light dot for the short vowel sound *ĕ* and a heavier dot for the long vowel sound *ae;* a light dash for the short vowel sound *ŭ* and a heavier dash for the long vowel sound *oe*. Compare the vowel signs in the following pairs of outlines: $\vert$ *date,* $\vert$ *debt;* $\diagdown$ *poach,* $\vert$ *touch;* $\vert$ *stay,* $\vert$ *set;* $\diagdown$ *soap,* $\diagdown$ *sup.*

A further study of the six outlines given above will strengthen your appreciation of the fact that shorthand outlines are written by sound. The vowel sound *ŭ* is represented in different ways in the spelling of the words *up, touch,* and *judge,* but in the shorthand outlines it is represented in one way only, by the light dash, written in the middle position close to the stroke, as:

$\diagdown$ $\vert$ $\vert$

The consonant sound *j* is represented in two ways in the longhand spelling of the word *judge,* but in the shorthand outline it is represented in one way only—by the stroke $\diagup$ *jay,* as $\vert$

In the spelling of the word *debt* there is a *b,* but there is no such consonant in the shorthand outline, which represents only the sounds of the word, namely *d ĕ t,* as:

$\vert$

PRACTICE FOUR (Key on p. 130)
Read and copy several times

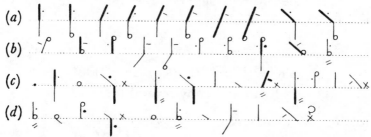

(a)

(b)

(c)

(d)

Curved Downstrokes

The following table gives the signs for six more consonant strokes, all curves and all written *downwards*.

Sign	Letter	Name	As in the outlines
╲	f	ef	face, fed
╲	v	vee	vote, save
(	th (light)	ith	thud, both
(	TH (heavy)	thee	they, bathe
⌡	sh	ish	show, shade
⌡	zh	zhee	usual, usually (Short Form)

Study and copy these strokes and outlines. You will see that, as with the straight downstrokes, the first stroke of the above outlines rests on the line. You will notice also that the Circle S is written inside curves.

The light strokes should be written very lightly, with only a slight additional pressure for the heavier strokes.

Although the pairs of vowel signs and consonant strokes are sometimes referred to as "light" and "heavy," the "heavy" sign or stroke is not really heavy: it is merely less light than the light strokes, which should be extremely fine.

PRACTICE FIVE (Key on p. 130)
Read and copy several times

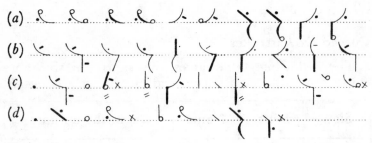

Short Forms

To be copied and memorized:

as/has, for, have, that, you, thank/thanked, think, publish/published/public.

Tick The

Because the word *the* is the most common word in the language, it is important that the shorthand writer should be able to represent it rapidly in all cases. Therefore, in addition to the dot it may be represented in phrases by a small tick, written either upwards or downwards, to give a sharp angle, but always in the direction / It is written after another sign, but never before a sign, nor when standing alone. In these cases the dot is used. Note the use of the tick *the* in the following phrases: of the, to the, for the, have the, to have the, that the, think the, publish *the,* ⟍ *pay the,* ⌐ *touch the,* ⟍ *paid the,* ⌐ *does the,* ⟍ *has the,* ⟍ *is the.*

Phrases

Read and copy:

⟍ *for you,* ⟍ *that you,* ⟍ *for it,* ⟍ *to think (or to thank),* ⟍ *thank you,* ⌐ *as it is,* ℓ *is that,* ℓ *is that you.*

It is worth repeating here that it is the *first* sign in a phrase that is written in its correct position in relation to the line of writing. Compare ⟍ *thank you,* with ⟍ *to thank;* and ⟍ *that you,* with ℓ *is that you.*

Circle S is added to Short Forms in the same way as to other strokes, as: ⟍ *thanks,* ⟍ *thinks,* ⟍ *publishes.*

Punctuation

The punctuation signs used in Pitmans Shorthand are:

Longhand: .   ,   ;   :   ?   — (dash)   - (hyphen)
Shorthand: ×   ,   ;   :   ⌀   ⟍   ＝

PRACTICE SIX (Key on p. 130)
Read and copy several times

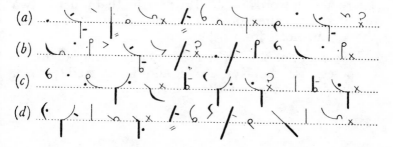

(a)

(b)

(c)

(d)

PRACTICE SEVEN (Key on p. 131)

Write in shorthand (from dictation if possible)

(*a*) Is that a photo of the judge? Does the judge think it is his set? Has Joe paid for the set?

(*b*) Thank you for the boat. It is such a safe boat.

(*c*) Does Ted fetch it for you? The photo shows up the face. The judge is to publish it to-day.

FACILITY DRILL TWO

Using the method suggested for Drill One, page 5, write the following drills very many times. While writing keep in mind that the purpose of such drill is to increase the speed and the ease with which you write. Do not write leisurely or laboriously, but try rather to get the feeling of facility and rapidity into your writing.

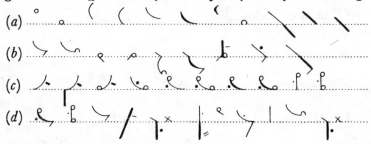

Dictation Test One

Perhaps you have a friend who will dictate to you. If so, turn to the key to *Practice Three* on page 130, and take down the exercise in your shorthand notebook. There are 49 words in it. Try to write them first in two minutes, and after practice in 1½ minutes. You can check your notes from page 5.

If you cannot have the services of a friend for dictation purposes, use the Key as an additional facility drill. Remember always to write lightly.

LESSON THREE

Horizontal Strokes

The twelve stroke consonants that you have learned so far have been written downwards. In this Lesson you will learn five stroke consonants which are written from left to right, as shown in the following table:

Sign	Letter	Name	As in the outlines
---→	k	kay	⌐ case, ⌐ take
—	g	gay	— gay, ⌐ get
⌒	m	em	⌒ may, ⌒ make
⌣	n	en	⌣ no, ⌣ name
⌣	ng	ing	⌣ making, ⌣ taking

Study and copy these strokes and outlines. Then practise the following outline drills, writing each outline several times:

Outline Drill

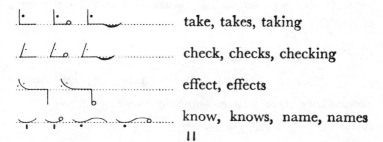

take, takes, taking

check, checks, checking

effect, effects

know, knows, name, names

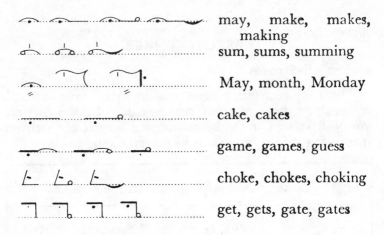

may, make, makes, making

sum, sums, summing

May, month, Monday

cake, cakes

game, games, guess

choke, chokes, choking

get, gets, gate, gates

PRACTICE EIGHT (Key on p. 131)
Read and copy several times

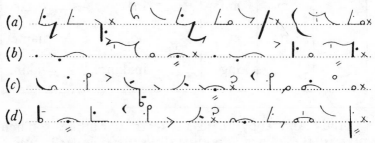

(a)

(b)

(c)

(d)

You will see from the outlines used above that when a horizontal stroke is followed by a downstroke it is the downstroke that rests on the line, as: ⌣ *enough*, ⌐ *get*, ⌢ *month*, ⌐ *Monday*. This ensures a neat alignment of outlines.

Circle S Between Strokes

When Circle S is used between two straight stroke consonants it is written outside the angle, as: ⌐ *custom*, ⌐ *desk*, ⌐ *beset*, ⌐ *gusset*.

You have already seen that Circle S is written inside curves, and this applies whether the curve stands alone or is joined to another stroke, as: ⌇⌇ *face*, ⌇⌇ *facing*, ⌇⌇ *sense*, ⌇⌇ *sensing*, ⌇⌇ *casing*, ⌇⌇ *musty.*

When S is joined to single straight strokes it is written in a direction opposite to that in which the hands of the clock move, namely ⌇⌇ , so that it is written on the right-hand side of straight downstrokes and on the upper side of straight horizontal strokes, as: ⌇⌇ *space*, ⌇⌇ *set*, ⌇⌇ *such*, ⌇⌇ *does*, ⌇⌇ *case*, ⌇⌇ *soak.*

Short Forms

To be copied and memorized:

⌇⌇ *I/eye*, ⌇⌇ *on*, ⌇⌇ *but*, ⌇⌇ *much*, ⌇⌇ *which*, ⌇⌇ *in/any*, ⌇⌇ *thing*, ⌇⌇ *anything*, ⌇⌇ *nothing*, ⌇⌇ *something.*

Phrases

To be copied several times:

⌇⌇ *I thank you*, ⌇⌇ *I think that*, ⌇⌇ *I know*, ⌇⌇ *I know that*, ⌇⌇ *in the*, ⌇⌇ *in it*, ⌇⌇ *it is (has) the*, ⌇⌇ *which is (has)*, ⌇⌇ *which is (has) the*, ⌇⌇ *I take*, ⌇⌇ *to take*, ⌇⌇ *to get*, ⌇⌇ *you may*, ⌇⌇ *you may have*, ⌇⌇ *may be*, ⌇⌇ *it may be*, ⌇⌇ *of the month*, ⌇⌇ *on Monday*, ⌇⌇ *on Sunday*, ⌇⌇ *on which*, ⌇⌇ *on the*, ⌇⌇ *but the.*

Note the slight change of direction of the signs for *on* and *but* in the phrases: ⌇⌇ *on the*, ⌇⌇ *but the.*

14

Read and copy several times

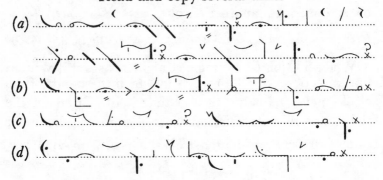

(a)

(b)

(c)

(d)

PRACTICE TEN (Key on p. 131)

Write in Shorthand (from dictation if possible)

(a) They said that they may make the change on Monday but I think that they may have to make some change on Sunday. They have enough sense to make the change.

(b) I think that you may have to change some of the names on the case.

(c) I have to take that set of photos to Joe. Ted may get something published.

(d) Have you anything for May to take in the case? I have nothing to-day.

FACILITY DRILL THREE

It will be very much to your advantage to develop speed writing ability while you are learning the rules of the system, and for this reason you are advised to practise these facility drills conscientiously, writing as quickly as you can, while keeping your writing neat and clear. Remember always to write lightly and to hold your pen lightly. The nib of the pen should be fine but flexible. If it is impossible for you to use a pen, be sure to keep the point of your pencil well sharpened.

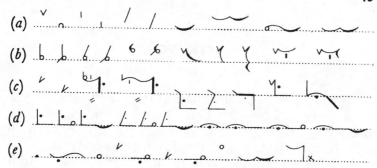

Note: Keep the difference in slope very clear in such pairs of forms as: ..ᒃ... *it is,* and ..ᒪ.. *which is;* ..ᐟ.. *to take,* and ..ᐳ.. *to check.*

There are fifty outlines in the above drills, representing 78 words. Practise until you can write them within two minutes.

Dictation Test Two

There are sixty words in the following test. If possible, have it dictated to you at 30 words a minute, that is, within two minutes. The test is marked off in ten's for easy timing. If you are unable to write the test from dictation, turn to the Key on p. 132 and copy the short-hand several times.

May said that Ted is making some changes in the[10] names. The names may be published in the *Echo* on[20] Monday. Sunday is the day on which it may be[30] published. May I publish any of that page? I have[40] set up some of it, but I think that you[50] may publish it. It is the custom to check it.[60]

LESSON FOUR

Vowel Signs

Of the twelve vowel signs in Pitmans Shorthand you have learned four—the light dot for *ĕ* and the heavier dot for *ae;* the light dash for *ŭ* and the heavier dash for *oe.* It is desirable and helpful in the early stages of shorthand writing to show all the vowels in an outline but, with experience in reading and writing and with increasing familiarity with outlines, it becomes less necessary to insert vowel signs. For instance, if you now see the outlines ⟍ and ⟍ you will have no difficulty in recognizing them as representing *paid* and *page.*

You will find, therefore, that in the practice material in this Lesson and future Lessons those outlines with which you should be thoroughly familiar do not show all the vowel signs. New outlines will, however, show vowel signs.

Further, when you are writing Facility Drills or writing from dictation it is seldom necessary to show many vowels. Most phrases require no vowel signs.

Try reading the following shorthand, which has very few vowel signs in it.

PRACTICE ELEVEN (Key on p. 132)
Read and copy several times

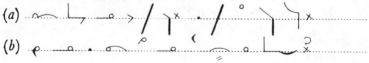

First Place Vowels

The four vowels you have used up to this stage are all written in the middle position, close to the stroke. This middle position is known as the second position, and the vowel signs for *ĕ*, *ŭ*, *ae*, and *oe* are referred to as second-place vowels.

There are also four first-place vowels and four third-place vowels. In this Lesson the first-place vowels are taught. These, as you might expect, are written in the first position, namely, near the beginning of a stroke. Carefully study the following outlines:

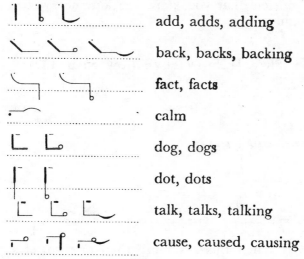

	add, adds, adding
	back, backs, backing
	fact, facts
	calm
	dog, dogs
	dot, dots
	talk, talks, talking
	cause, caused, causing

From these outlines you will see that the vowel signs are again in pairs of two dots and two dashes—a light dot for the short vowel sound of *ă*, a slightly heavier dot for the long vowel sound of *ah;* a light dash for the short vowel sound of *ŏ*, a slightly heavier dash for the long vowel sound of *aw*.

Position Writing

You will have noted also that all these outlines are written above the line. Just as there are three positions for placing vowel signs in relation to the stroke, so there are three positions for placing outlines in relation to the line—above the line, on the line, and through the line. These are known as the first, second, and third positions respectively.

Outlines in which the first vowel sign is a first-place vowel are written in the first position—that is, above the line. Outlines in which the first vowel sign is a second-place vowel are written in the second position—that is, on the line.

Read and copy the outlines given above many times until you feel that you know the four new vowel signs thoroughly.

PRACTICE TWELVE (Key on p. 132)
Read and copy several times

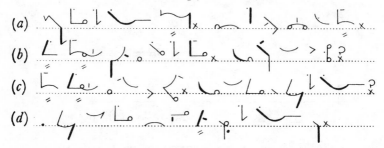

Note: When there is more than one vowel sign in an outline, it is the position of the first vowel sign that governs the position of the outline. In the outlines for the words *ago, among,* the first vowel sign is written in the first position and the outlines are written in the first position, above the line, as: ‾‾‾‾ ‾‾‾‾ In the outlines for the words *coda, coma,* the first vowel sign is written in the second position, and the outlines are written in the second position, resting on the line, as: ‾‾‾‾ ‾‾‾‾.

Compare ‾‾‾‾ *comma* with ‾‾‾ *coma.*

Downward R

The downward curve ⌐ represents the sound of R and is called AR. Read and copy the following outlines many times:

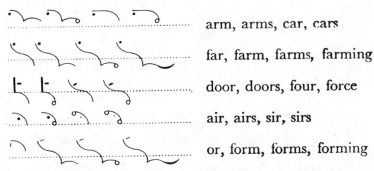

arm, arms, car, cars

far, farm, farms, farming

door, doors, four, force

air, airs, sir, sirs

or, form, forms, forming

Short Forms

To be practised and memorized:

⌐ he, ⌐ though, ⌐ them, ⌐ shall, ⌐ wish, ⌐ usual/usually, ⌐ can, ⌐ come, ⌐ exchange/exchanged, ⌐ and.

Note that ⌐ and is written upwards.

Phrases

Read and copy:

⌐ as (has) he, ⌐ that he, ⌐ that he is (has), ⌐ is he, ⌐ that he can, ⌐ though the, ⌐ to them, ⌐ I shall, ⌐ I shall have, ⌐ I wish, ⌐ to exchange, ⌐ to come, ⌐ I think you can, ⌐ I can, ⌐ I exchange(d), ⌐ I get, ⌐ I got, ⌐ I am, ⌐ I may, ⌐ and the, ⌐ and is (as, has), ⌐ that such.

You will see from the above phrases that the sign for I is abbreviated before ⌐ k, ⌐ g, and ⌐ m.

PRACTICE THIRTEEN (Key on p. 132)
Read and copy several times

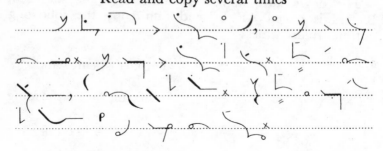

PRACTICE FOURTEEN (Key on p. 133)
Write in Shorthand (from dictation if possible)

Sir, May I have a cheque for the tax on the four-door*
car you bought off Jack Dawson some days ago? The
fact is that I have to pay this tax to the bank on Monday.
I spoke to Jack to-day, and I know that he thinks that
the car is a fair exchange. As he is a fair judge of cars,
I think you can take it that such is the case. I am,

* A hyphen is represented by two little dashes, as

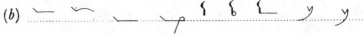

FACILITY DRILL FOUR

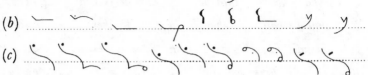

LESSON FIVE

Omission of Vowels

As stated in Lesson Four, it is seldom necessary to show vowel signs in outlines with which you are familiar. You should find it quite easy to read the following shorthand, in which very few vowel signs are inserted.

PRACTICE FIFTEEN (Key on p. 133)
Read and copy several times

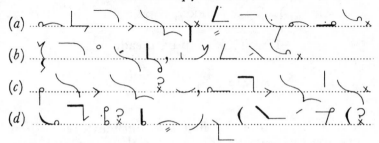

Third Place Vowels

The four third-place vowels are written in the third position, near the end of a stroke. Carefully study the following outlines:

   sit, city, cities

   each, piece/peace, these

   into

   chew, chews/choose, choosing

From these outlines you will note that, as in the case of the first and second-place vowel signs, there are two dots and two dashes, written in the third position—a light dot for the short vowel sound of ĭ, a slightly heavier dot for the long vowel sound of *ee;* a light dash for the short vowel sound ŏŏ, a slightly heavier dash for the long vowel sound of ōō.

You will note also that the outlines are written in the third position, namely, through the line. Remember to apply the rule taught in Lesson Four—the first vowel sign in an outline governs the position of the outline. Read and copy the following outlines, and carefully note the positions in relation to the line:

body, copy

muddy, meadow

business, visit

You will see that the first two outlines are written above the line because the first vowel sign in each case is a first-place vowel. The second two are written on the line because the first vowel sign is a second-place vowel, and the last two outlines are written through the line because the first vowel sign is a third-place vowel.

PRACTICE SIXTEEN (Key on p. 133)

Read and copy several times

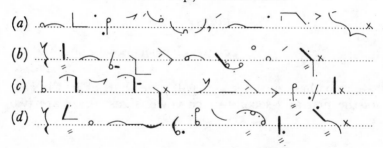

(a)

(b)

(c)

(d)

Third Place Vowels Between Strokes

When a third-place vowel comes between two stroke consonants, it is written in the third position before the second of the two strokes.

There is no third position for outlines which contain only horizontal strokes. Such horizontal outlines are written on the line for both second and third positions.

Carefully study the following outlines, which illustrate these two points, and then copy the outlines several times:

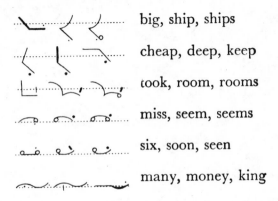

big, ship, ships

cheap, deep, keep

took, room, rooms

miss, seem, seems

six, soon, seen

many, money, king

Strokes S and Z

The common sounds of *s* and *z* are represented by the downstrokes ⟩ **and** ⟩ respectively, as well as by the small circle. The circle is the more generally used form, but occasionally it is necessary to use the stroke in order to show a vowel sign—or to indicate that there is a vowel without actually showing the sign. Consider the following outlines: ⟩ *us,* ⟩ *say,* ⟩ *so.*

These outlines consist only of the sound of *s* and a vowel. The stroke must be used, as the circle would not provide a suitable place to write the vowel sign. Compare ⟩ *say* with *same,* and *ask* with *sack.*

Initial Z

The stroke)̣ z is always used at the beginning of an outline:)̣ *zoo,*)̣ *zenith,*)̣ *zigzag.*

PRACTICE SEVENTEEN (Key on p. 133)
Read and copy several times

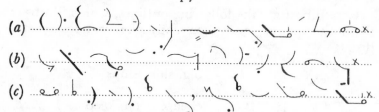

(a)

(b)

(c)

Short Forms

To be practised and memorized:

— *go,* — *give/given,* ⌒ *me,* ⌒ *him,*) *was,* ⌒ *expect/expected,* ⌒ *manufacture/manufactured.*

Derivative Short Forms

⌒ *going,* ⌣ *having,* ⌣ *being.*

Phrases

Read and copy:

) *I was,* ↓ *it was,* ⌒ *I expect/ed,* ⌒ *I manufacture/d,* ⌒ *to expect,* ⊤ *to go,* — *to give,* ⌒ *to me,* ⌒ *to him,* ⌣ *for me,* ⌣ *for him,* ⌐ *I ask,* ⌣ *if you can,* ⌒ *for some,* ⌣ *I have seen.*

Note: The vowel is always inserted in the phrase ⊤ *to go,* and also in such phrases as ⌒ *to him,* ⌣ *for him.* Compare: ⌒ *to me,* ⌣ *for me.*

PRACTICE EIGHTEEN (Key on p. 133)
Read and copy several times

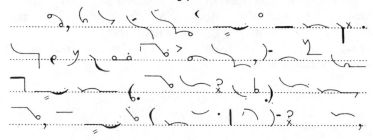

PRACTICE NINETEEN (Key on p. 134)
Write in shorthand (from dictation if possible)

You may wish to know that I am going to move into a big office soon. The office has six rooms, and is cheap. It is in the City.

It was the City office of Messrs. King and Smith but that firm appears to have given up the manufacture of office desks. I wish to have the space, as since I bought up the business of Messrs. Dickson and Box I have no room to keep the many books of the firm.

FACILITY DRILL FIVE

Facility drills are designed not only to promote speed but to give control. It is suggested, therefore, that you now practise the following drills, which are specially aimed at improving manual control. You will perhaps find it difficult at first to write a complete line of *o*'s and *a*'s, but after practice you will find it quite easy.

(a) oooooooooooooooooooooooooooooooooo

(b) aaaaaaaaaaaaaaaaaaaaaaaaaaaaaa

(c) ʒ ʒ ʒ ʒ ʒ ʒ ʒ ʒ ʒ ʒ ʒ ʒ ʒ ʒ ʒ ʒ ʒ

REVISION ONE

You have now learnt the following twenty stroke consonants and the Circle s/z. You should at this stage be thoroughly familiar with these signs, both for reading and writing purposes. They are set out below for easy reference.

STRAIGHT DOWNSTROKES

╲ p ╲ b ╎ t ╎ d ╱ ch ╱ j.

CURVED DOWNSTROKES

╲ f ╲ v (ith (thee) s) z ╱ sh ╱ zh ⌒ ar.

HORIZONTAL STROKES

— k — g ⌢ m ⌣ n ⌣ ng.

CIRCLE S   A small circle, representing s or z, is written with the left motion to straight strokes, outside the angle formed by two straight strokes, and inside curves, as in: ℅ space, ℓ seats, a·a six, ⊥° tasks, ⊥° desks, ℒ safes, ⌒ seems.

VOWEL SIGNS   You should also be able to use, without hesitation, the following twelve vowel signs:

LIGHT DOTS
ă (1st Place)   ĕ (2nd Place)   ĭ (3rd Place)

HEAVIER DOTS
ah (1st Place)   ae (2nd Place)   ee (3rd Place)

LIGHT DASHES
ŏ (1st Place)   ŭ (2nd Place)   ŏŏ (3rd Place)

HEAVIER DASHES
aw (1st Place)   oe (2nd Place)   ōō (3rd Place)

The following two sentences provide memory aids for these vowel signs:

SHORT VOWEL SOUNDS
thAt pEn Is nOt mUch gOOd.

LONG VOWEL SOUNDS
pA, mAY wE All gO tOO?

While you should know unhesitatingly where to place the vowel signs, however, it is not as a rule necessary to insert these signs in familiar outlines when writing in context.

Short Forms

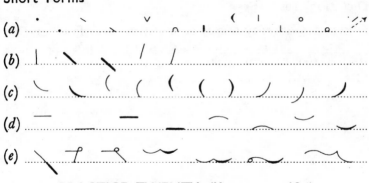

PRACTICE TWENTY (Key on p. 134)
Read and copy several times

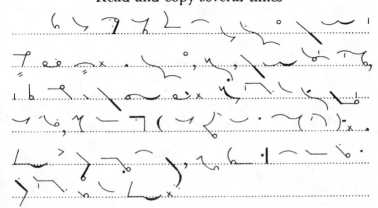

28

PRACTICE TWENTY-ONE (Key on p. 134)
Write in Shorthand

As you know, I wish to get six oak desks[10] but so far I have seen nothing big enough. I[20] saw Eric and Tom at the shop to-day, and Eric[30] said that he thinks Messrs. Beatty & Sons manufacture office[40] desks of the shape I wish to have. They make[50] these desks in four shades of oak. May I ask[60] if you can take a day off to visit the[70] showrooms of the firm for me? I wish to have[80] the desks soon as I am moving into the City[90] office on the sixth of May. (96 words)

Dictation Test Three

Practice Twenty-one is counted in ten's for dictation purposes. There are 96 words in it. If possible, have it dictated to you in three minutes, and check your attempt with the shorthand Key on p. 134.

LESSON SIX

Upstrokes

In this Lesson you are introduced to four consonant strokes that are written *upwards*.

Sign	Letter	Name	As in the outlines
⟋	l	el	⟍ self, ⟍ pull
⟋	w	way	⟋ way, ⟨ watch
⟋	y	yay	⟋ yes, ⟋ youth
⟋	h	hay	⟍ hope, ⟍ happy

Read and copy these outlines several times. You will notice that the upstrokes, like the downstrokes, may be written in three positions and that there are three places for vowel signs.

The position of the vowel sign is counted from the *beginning* of the stroke, whether the stroke is written downwards, upwards, or horizontally, as:

Note the positions of the outlines and of the vowel signs in the following examples:

First Position Outlines and Vowel Signs

⟍ bar, ⌐ dock, ⟍ far, ⌐ cause, ⌒ gnaw, ⟨ watch, ⌐ law.

Second Position Outlines and Vowel Signs

⟍ bare, ⌐ duck, ⟍ fare, ⌐ case, ⟍ know, ⟨ weighed, ⌐ low.

29

Third Position Outlines and Vowel Signs

⟍ *beer,* ⌐ *Dick,* ⟍ *fear,* ⟿ *keys,* ⟿ *knee,*

⟋ *weep,* ⌐ *Leigh.*

PRACTICE TWENTY-TWO (Key on p. 134)
Read and copy several times

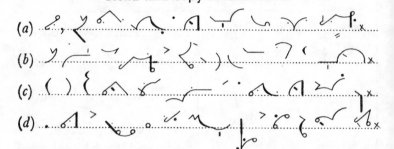

(a) ....×

(b) ....×

(c) ....×

(d) ....×

Diphthongs IE and OI

In addition to the twelve vowel signs of Pitmans Shorthand there are four diphthong signs, representing the four diphthong sounds heard in the sentence: I nOW enjOY mUsic.

The signs for two of these—‿ˇ *ie* and ‿⌐ *oi*—are illustrated in the following outlines:

⌣ ⌣ ⌣ ⌣ ⌣	my, mile, miles, smiles
⌢ ⌢ ⌢ ⌢ ⌢	lie, life, lives, lively
⌐ ⌐ ⌐	sigh, sighed/side, sides
⟍ ⟍ ⟍	boy/buoy, boys/buoys, boyhood
⟋ ⟋ ⟋	oil, oils, oiling

Note: The diphthong sign for *oi* may be joined to stroke *l* at the beginning of an outline, as: ⟋ *oil.*

Triphones

When another vowel follows a diphthong it is represented by adding a little tick to the diphthong sign, as in the outlines:

buy, buyer, buyers, buying

boy, boyish, buoyant

PRACTICE TWENTY-THREE (Key on p. 135)
Read and copy several times

Short Forms

To be copied and memorized:

all, although, too/two, we, special/ specially, speak, should, January, manufacturer.

Note: also.

Phrases

Read and copy:

all the, we have, we think that, we can, we shall, we shall be, we hope, I hope, and we, should be, I think you should, *to speak,* ⟍ *in January,* ⌢ *I will be,* ⌢ *you will be,* ⌣ *it will be,* ⋀ *which will be,* ⟨ *so that.*

You will observe that in the phrases ⌢ *you will,* ⌣ *it will,* etc. the *w* has been omitted, stroke *l* only being used for the word *will;* and that in the phrases ⟍ *I hope,* ⌣ *we hope,* the *h* has been omitted, stroke *p* only being used for the word *hope.* The omission of the consonant aids speed writing, and the resultant phrases are very clear and distinctive.

The shorthand writer is advised to use all the phrases taught but to be wary at this stage of inventing phrases and of joining too many outlines together.

PRACTICE TWENTY-FOUR (Key on p. 135)
Read and copy several times

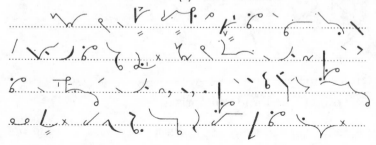

PRACTICE TWENTY-FIVE (Key on p. 135)
Write in shorthand (from dictation if possible)

We think that it will be wise for you to have some voice in the size and type of the special signs which will be on show in the windows in July. If you leave it all to the family to decide, you may dislike the signs they choose, although you will have to pay heavily for them. We think you should go to the showrooms of the manufacturers and choose the design and colour, as the choice of sign is likely to affect the July sales.

FACILITY DRILL SIX

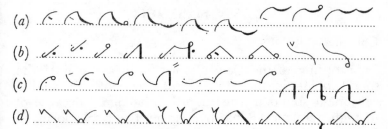

Dictation Test Four

The following test consists of 50 words. Write it in shorthand from dictation several times, and see whether you can write the 50 words in one minute. Check your shorthand from the Key on p. 135.

We thank you for mailing the details of the ladies'[10] watches. We have looked at these details, and we should[20] like to buy a dozen of the Type A watches[30] and also two dozen of Type B. We hope you[40] can dispatch the watches early in the month of July.[50]

LESSON SEVEN

Consonant R

According to the Dewey word frequency count* the sound of R is the third most frequently occurring consonant sound in the English language. Because of its high frequency R has been given two stroke forms in Pitmans Shorthand, thus ensuring easy joinings in all cases and providing the means of indicating a vowel without actually writing it.

The curved downstroke ⌒ AR you already know. The second sign is a straight upstroke ╱ called RAY, and its use is illustrated in the outlines: ╱ rate, ⌒ wrong, ╱ carry, ⌐ charge.

Downward AR ⌒ is used when a word begins or ends with the sound of a vowel followed by R, as in the outlines: ⌒ air, ⌒ early, ⌒ car, ⌒ fear.

Upstroke RAY ╱ is used when a word begins or ends with the sound of R followed by a vowel, as in the outlines: ╱ red, ╱ reach, ⌒ marry, ⌒ memory.

The outlines ⌒ air and ╱ ray are useful memory aids.

RAY is generally used for the medial sound of R, as: ⌒ authority, ⌒ party, ⌐ charge.

---

* Relative Frequency of English Speech Sounds, Dewey: Harvard Study in Education IV.

PRACTICE TWENTY-SIX (Key on p. 136)

Read and copy several times

Vowel Indication

The strokes and Circle for the consonants S and Z, and the two stroke forms for the consonant R, provide very good examples of how a vowel may be indicated or suggested without actually writing it in the outline.

Compare the outlines: *less,* *lessee;* *sack,* *ask.*

When you see the final circle in *less* you know that the word must end with the sound of S/Z, as *less;* whereas when you see the stroke at the end of *lessee* you expect a final vowel, as *lessee.* The outline *sack* clearly indicates that the word begins with the sound of S, while the outline *ask* suggests that there is a vowel before the S, as *ask.*

Similarly, you know that there is a final vowel in the outline *carry,* even though the vowel is not inserted, and from the outline *car* you can at once infer that the word ends with the sound of R, as *car.*

In order to provide facile and legible outlines, however, R is always written downwards before stroke M, without regard to vowels, as: *arm,* *room,* *farm.*

When a word begins with S-vowel-S, the stroke S is

written first and then the circle, as: ⌐ *size,* ⌐ *society,* ⌐ *saucer.*

PRACTICE TWENTY-SEVEN (Key on p. 136)
Read and copy several times

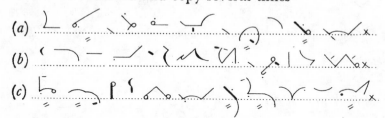

Diphthongs OW and EW

The signs ʌ OW and ⌒ EW complete your knowledge of the four diphthong signs. As in the case of the signs ˅ IE and ⁊ OI, a small tick is added to represent an additional vowel sound. Read and copy the following outlines several times:

	out, south, house, housing
	announce, announcing
	power, powers, tower, towers
	new, news, newer
	view, views, few, fewer

Note: The diphthong signs ʌ OW and ⌒ EW are joined finally when convenient: ⟍ *bough,* ⟍ *few,* ⟍ *view,* ⟍ *value.*

Short Forms

To be copied and memorized:

ʌ *how,* ⟍ *your,* ⟍ *year,* / *are,* / *our/hour,* ⟍ *from,* ⟍ *very.*

Phrases

Read and copy:

we are, _you are,_ _for your,_ _in your,_
for the year, _in the year,_ _from the,_ _and_
from the, _to our,_ _two hours,_ _such as,_
we are sorry, _we are very sorry._

PRACTICE TWENTY-EIGHT (Key on p. 136)
Read and copy several times

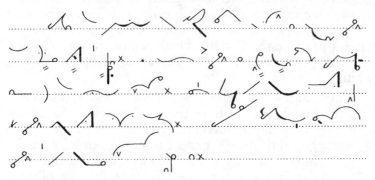

PRACTICE TWENTY-NINE (Key on p. 136)
Write in shorthand (from dictation if possible)

Have you read the new book *History In Your Service* by Harry Reason? I am reading it now and am enjoying it. It is published by Messrs. New & Dawson. A book I wish to read if I can borrow a copy is *How History Affects To-day* by Leslie Powers. Our Society hopes to have a visit in March from some authority on History, such as Powers, and we hope that he will speak for two hours.

38

FACILITY DRILL SEVEN

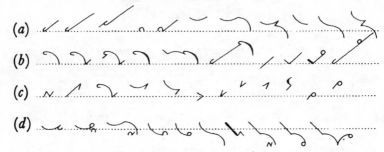

(a)

(b)

(c)

(d)

Dictation Test Five (Key on p. 137)

The following test is counted in ten's for dictation. There are in it 80 words. See whether you can, at a first attempt, write this at 40 words a minute. If not, perhaps you can have it dictated to you several times until you can write it at that speed. It is very important to train yourself to write fluently from the early stages. If you practise the Facility Drills regularly you will find them a great help in the cultivation of speed writing ability.

I am taking the family south for a few days[10] early in July, and I hope to have the car[20] ready by Saturday. We have very happy memories of our[30] visit to the south a year ago, and so we[40] expect to enjoy our stay by the sea. I think[50] that we shall be away from our house for a[60] month, and you may like to have the use of[70] the house for that month. Does it appeal to you?[80]

LESSON EIGHT

SWAY Circle

The sound of SW at the beginning of a word is easily and quickly represented by the use of the large SWAY Circle. Read and copy the following outlines:

sweet, sweets, sweetly, sweetness

switch, switches, Swede

swim, swims, swimming

swell, swells, swelling

swear, swears, swore

You will see that the SWAY Circle, like the Circle S, is written inside curves and with the left motion when added to straight strokes. It is, however, used *initially only*.

SEZ Circle

When the sound of SEZ (light or heavy) occurs in the middle or at the end of a word, the large SEZ Circle may be used. Read and copy the following outlines:

piece, pieces, discuss, discusses

case, cases, accessory, accessories

niece, nieces, necessary, necessity

success, successfully

The SEZ Circle is also written inside curves and with the left motion when added to straight strokes. It is used medially and finally, *not* initially.

39

The SWAY and SEZ Circles should be clearly distinguished in size from the small Circle S. Compare ⌠ *seat* with ⌠ *sweet*, and ⌐⌐ *service* with ⌐⌐ *services*.

PRACTICE THIRTY (Key on p. 137)
Read and copy several times

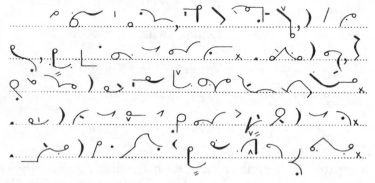

Vocalization of SEZ Circle

When a vowel sound other than *ĕ* occurs between the two *s*'s (or *z*'*z*) the vowel sign (or diphthong) may be written inside the large circle, as in the outlines:

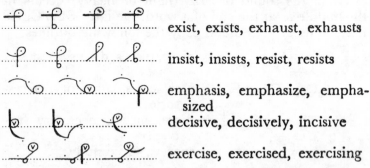

exist, exists, exhaust, exhausts

insist, insists, resist, resists

emphasis, emphasize, emphasized

decisive, decisively, incisive

exercise, exercised, exercising

A Circle S may be added to the SEZ Circle, as in the outlines: ⌐⌐ *success*, ⌐⌐ *successes*, ⌐⌐ *emphasize*, ⌐⌐ *emphasizes*.

PRACTICE THIRTY-ONE (Key on p. 137)

Read and copy several times

Termination -ous

Stroke S is used finally when a word ends with a diphthong followed by *-ous,* as in the outlines: *fatuous,* *tenuous,* *pious.*

It is seldom necessary in speed writing to insert the triphone sign in such cases, as the use of the stroke S suggests that there may be a triphone. Compare, for instance, the outlines: *pies,* *pious;* *tennis,* *tenuous.*

Short Forms

To be practised and memorized:

why, *those/thyself,* *this,* *thus,* *had,* *do,* *different/difference,* *February.*

Circles SWAY and SEZ in Phrases

The large circles give very brief and legible forms when used in phrases. You will see that in the following phrases the SWAY Circle is used for *as-w(e)* and the SEZ Circle for *(a)s-s:*

as we think, *as we can,* *as we are,* *as we shall*

42

be, ⟨shorthand⟩ *as we do,* ⟨shorthand⟩ *as we know,* ⟨shorthand⟩ *as well as,* ⟨shorthand⟩ *as well as possible,* ⟨shorthand⟩ *as soon as.* ⟨shorthand⟩ *as soon as possible,* ⟨shorthand⟩ *this is,* ⟨shorthand⟩ *as is,* ⟨shorthand⟩ *is as,* ⟨shorthand⟩ *this city,* ⟨shorthand⟩ *on this side.*

These phrases are very useful and should be practised many times, as also should the following:

⟨shorthand⟩ *in those,* ⟨shorthand⟩ *in those days,* ⟨shorthand⟩ *this time,* ⟨shorthand⟩ *in this way,* ⟨shorthand⟩ *I had,* ⟨shorthand⟩ *we do,* ⟨shorthand⟩ *we have had,* ⟨shorthand⟩ *in February,* ⟨shorthand⟩ *it is necessary.*

PRACTICE THIRTY-TWO (Key on p. 137)
Read and copy several times

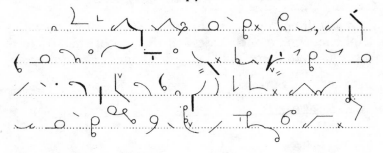

PRACTICE THIRTY-THREE (Key on p. 138)
Write in shorthand (from dictation if possible)

From this same window I have seen the different seasons of the year. Now in this autumn month I watch the swallows swoop and sweep, in a sweet hurry to leave our shores and seek new joys far away. In the lovely month of July masses of roses peeped in at the window. Now those roses are but memories, and to-day the red leaves lie thick on the path. Soon it will be necessary for me to leave this seat at the window, and go outside to sweep up the piles of leaves.

FACILITY DRILL EIGHT

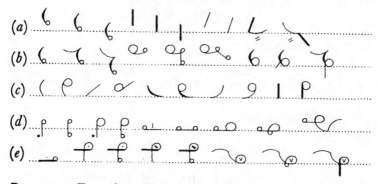

(a)

(b)

(c)

(d)

(e)

Dictation Test Six (Key on p. 138)

Try to write these eighty words in two minutes

Messrs. Swanson & Swells,
14 Lake Success Road, Reading.

Sirs,[10] Thank you for the details of the cases of china[20] which you are selling off this February. These should suit[30] our purposes, and we attach a schedule of the items[40] we should like to receive as soon as possible.

Have[50] you any odd cups and saucers as well as the[60] special sets of china? If you have, we should like[70] six cases in different sizes and colours.

We are, Yours,[80]

LESSON NINE

Stee and Ster Loops

You have learned the rules for the use of the small and large Circles, and in this Lesson you are introduced to the very useful small and large Loops. Read and copy the following outlines:

set, state, states

seal, steal/steel, steals/steels

seem/seam, steam, steams

cause, cost, costs

day, days/daze, dazed

ways, waste, wastes

lease, list, lists

test, tests, testing

mass, massed, master

masters, masterpiece, masterpieces

From a study of these outlines you will see that a small loop is used to represent the sound of ST or ZD, and that a large loop represents the syllable STER. You will see also that the loops are written inside curves and with the left motion when added to straight strokes, just as are the circles.

The STEE loop may be used at the beginning, in the middle, or at the end of an outline.

The STER loop is not used at the beginning of an outline; it is used only medially and finally. Note the outline ⁓ *sterling*.

Circle S is added after the small and large loops, as in the outlines: ⁎ *tests*, ⁎ *lists*, ⁎ *masters*, ⁎ *coasters*.

Note the distinctive outlines: ⁎ *cost*, ⁎ *caused*.

PRACTICE THIRTY-FOUR (Key on p. 138)
Read and copy several times

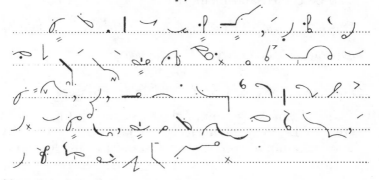

Vowel Indication

You will remember that the Circle and stroke forms of S are used to suggest the presence or absence of a vowel, as in the pairs of outlines: ⁎ *Sam*, ⁎ *Assam*; ⁎ *Jess*, ⁎ *Jessie*.

The STEE Loop and the separate Circle S and stroke T are similarly used, as in the pairs of outlines: ⁎ *dust*, ⁎ *dusty*, ⁎ *rust*, ⁎ *rusty*. Note also the use of the circle and stroke in the outlines ⁎ *beset*, ⁎ *deceit*, where a vowel comes between the *s* and the *t*.

PRACTICE THIRTY-FIVE (Key on p. 138)
Read and copy several times

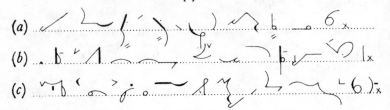

Short Forms

To be copied and memorized:

first, *most,* *next,* *there/their,* *inform/ informed,* *insurance,* *knowledge.*

Omission of a Word or a Syllable in Phrases

A good phrase combines clearness and distinctiveness with speed. Very often this combination is achieved by the omission of a word, as, for instance, in the following phrases:

for a time, *for the first time,* *first of all, right or wrong,* *yes or no,* *at a loss.*

Similarly the omission of a syllable very often results in a useful and distinctive phrase, as in:

this month, *next month,* *if possible, as soon as possible,* *it is possible.*

Practise these and the following phrases thoroughly, so that you can use them without any hesitation:

there is, *there is no,* *for their,* *those who are, we suggest,* *to suggest,* *I suggest,* *inform/ed you.*

PRACTICE THIRTY-SIX (Key on p. 139)
Read and copy several times

PRACTICE THIRTY-SEVEN (Key on p. 139)
Write in shorthand (from dictation if possible)

I am sorry that I am at a loss to inform you of the details of your insurance policy, as I have no knowledge of your taking out a policy on the date you state.

You must first of all look up the policy as soon as possible. The next step is for you to take the policy to your bank, if possible, and ask for their advice. I think it is possible that you will be paid a big sum of money.

FACILITY DRILL NINE

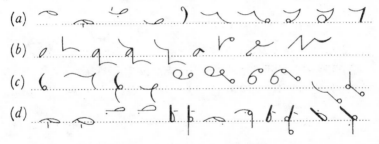

LESSON TEN

Halving of Strokes

The Halving Principle is a most useful time-saving device. By its use a stroke is written half its normal length to add the sound of T or D. Consider the following outlines:

wait/weight, waits/weights, heat, heats

note, notes, night, nights

late, let, light, lot

part, parts, start, starts

act, acts, good, goods

bad, bed, deed, deeds

In these outlines light strokes are halved in length for the addition of the light sound of T and heavy strokes for the heavy sound of D. Now consider the following outlines:

relate, relates, relating

method, methods

rapid, rapidly

rabbit, rabbits

In these outlines strokes are halved for either T or D. If you study the outlines closely you will observe that the rule is:

48

(1) In words of one syllable a light stroke is halved for T only and a heavy stroke is halved for D only.

Compare ⌐ *bat* with ⌐ *bad* and ⌐ *paid* with ⌐ *pat*.

(2) In words of more than one syllable strokes may be halved for either T or D, as in: ⌐ *rapid*, ⌐ *rabbit*, ⌐ *method*, ⌐ *epithet*.

(3) When a stroke has a finally joined diphthong sign it may be halved for either T or D, as in: ⌐ *about*, ⌐ *doubt*, ⌐ *night*.

Note: Strokes are not halved in length in those few cases where there is no angle sharp enough to show the difference in length, as, for instance, in the outlines: ⌐ *minute*, ⌐ *fact*, ⌐ *locate*. It will be quite apparent to you that if a half-length K were used after F or L the two strokes would merge, and the resultant outline would not be legible—and all shorthand is written to be read.

RAY standing by itself is not halved: ⌐ *right/write*, ⌐ *rates*, ⌐ *root*.

Half-length upstrokes and downstrokes are not written through the line. Note the position of the outlines: ⌐ *did*, ⌐ *doubt*, ⌐ *pit*.

PRACTICE THIRTY-EIGHT (Key on p. 139)
Read and copy several times

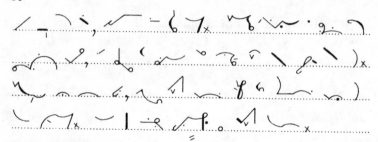

MD and ND

The strokes M and N are halved and thickened to add D, as in the outlines: ⌒ *made,* ⌒ *aimed,* ⌒ *amid;* ⌒ *end,* ⌒ *needs,* ⌒ *thousand.*

RD

Downward AR is halved and thickened to add D, as in the outlines: ⌒ *feared,* ⌒ *admired,* ⌒ *cards.*

LD

Stroke L is halved and thickened, and *written downwards* to add D, as in the outlines: ⌒ *old,* ⌒ *field,* ⌒ *failed.* There are no thick upstrokes in Pitmans Shorthand.

When a vowel comes between the R or L and the D, the separate strokes are written. Compare the outlines:

⌒ *marred* and ⌒ *married;* ⌒ *card* and ⌒ *carried;* ⌒ *fold* and ⌒ *followed;* ⌒ *veiled* and ⌒ *valued.*

-TED, -DED

The word-ending TED or DED is usually represented by half-length T or D, as in the outlines: ⌒ *wanted,* ⌒ *rated,* ⌒ *started,* ⌒ *ended,* ⌒ *padded.*

PRACTICE THIRTY-NINE (Key on p. 140)
Read and copy several times

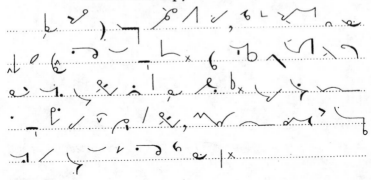

Short Forms

To be copied and memorized:

‿ *with,* ‿ *when,* ‒ *quite,* ‒ *could,* ‿ *sent,* (*without,* ‿ *never,* ‿ *November,* ⊁ *satisfactory,* ⊁ *unsatisfactory.*

Phrases

Read and copy:

‿ *if it,* ‿ *if it is,* ᴱ *with you,* ϵ *when you,* ‿ *to give you,* ‿ *could not,* ‿ *could not be,* ‿ *I could not,* ‿ *in November,* ‿ *I have never,* ‿ *it is not,* ⅊ *it is satisfactory,* ⅁ *I waited,* ‿ *I am writing,* ‿ *for some time,* ‿ *I have no doubt,* ‿ *there is no doubt,* ‿ *we send you,* ⁄ *we are sending you,* ⌐ *let you have.*

You will see that in the phrase ‿ *if it* the stroke is halved to add *it,* and that in the phrases ᴱ *with you,* ϵ *when you,* etc., the ‿ is turned on its side to give a rapidly written form.

PRACTICE FORTY (Key on p. 140)
Read and copy several times

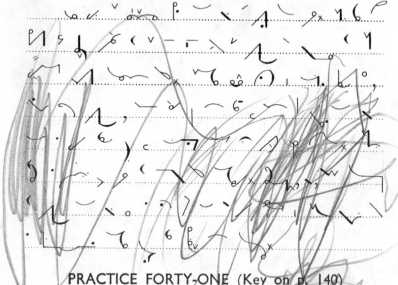

PRACTICE FORTY-ONE (Key on p. 140)
Write in shorthand (from dictation if possible)

I am writing to say that I am sorry you could not be with me when I visited the factory at East Fields to-day. The car could not wait, and I was forced to go without you. It is most satisfactory to report that all seemed to be operating smoothly, and that, in the view of experts, the new goods should be ready for the market by November at the latest. I was quite satisfied with all that I saw, and I have asked for a report to be sent to you as soon as possible.

FACILITY DRILL TEN

It is hoped that you are conscientiously practising these facility drills, writing lightly and rapidly and repeatedly, with the deliberate intention of increasing your speed writing ability. Remember that the light strokes **are** very light and that the heavier strokes require very little extra pressure.

(a)

(b)

(c)

(d)

REVISION TWO

On p. 26, Lesson Five, you were given a short revisionary Lesson. In this Tenth Lesson another short revision is provided, so that you may again consolidate what you have learned. In the course of Lessons Six to Ten you have been taught:

FIVE UPSTROKE CONSONANTS as used in the outlines: *law*, *way/weigh*, *youth*, *hope*, *rate*. (See p. 29 for note on the placing of vowel signs to downstrokes, upstrokes, and horizontal strokes.)

FOUR DIPHTHONG SIGNS (with corresponding Triphones) as used in the outlines: *by/buy*, *buyer*, *joy*, *joyous*, *few*, *fewer*, *cow*, *towel*.

TWO LARGE CIRCLES (SWAY and SEZ) as used in the outlines: *sweet*, *swift*, *pieces*, *necessary*, *exist*, *emphasize*, *emphasizes*. (See p. 41 for use of large circles in phrasing.)

TWO LOOPS (STEE and STER) as used in the outlines: *state*, *test*, *tests*, *staff*, *post*, *poster*, *posters*.

VOWEL INDICATION as illustrated in the contrasting outlines: *joys*, *joyous*; *tennis*, *tenuous*; *Sam*, *Assam*; *sack*, *ask;* ⌒ *lace,* ⌒ *lazy;* ⤳ *fuss,* ⤳ *fussy;* ⤳ *paste,* ⤳ *pasty;* ⌒ *mist,* ⌐ *misty.*

Note: Because a final vowel sign necessitates the use of a final stroke by which to place the sign, a final stroke is not halved in length when a vowel follows the T or D. The use of the stroke suggests, therefore, the presence of a vowel. Study the following pairs of outlines: ⤳ *fat,* ⤳ *fatty;* ⌐ *chat,* ⌐ *chatty;* | *dad,* | *daddy;* ⤳ *pit,* ⤳ *pity;* ⤳ *Tait,* ⤳ *potato.*

Short Forms

The following list provides a very useful Facility Drill

(a)

(b)

(c)

(d)

(e)

PRACTICE FORTY-TWO (Key on p. 140)

Read and copy several times

LESSON ELEVEN

Doubling of Strokes

You have learned that you may halve the length of a stroke to add the letter T or D; in this Lesson you learn that you may double the length of a stroke to add a syllable. Read the following outlines:

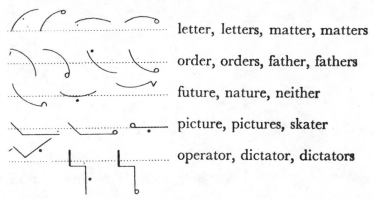

letter, letters, matter, matters

order, orders, father, fathers

future, nature, neither

picture, pictures, skater

operator, dictator, dictators

From these examples you will see that strokes have been doubled in length to add one of the syllables TR, DR, THr (heavy sound only) or TURE.

The Doubling Principle is applied to strokes in accordance with the following rules:

(1) Curves are doubled in length to add the above syllables, as in the outlines: ⟍ *father,* ⟋ *alter,* ⌢ *mother/mutter,* ⌢ *nature.*

(2) Straight strokes are doubled in length to add these syllables when the stroke follows another stroke or a circle, as in the outlines: ⟍ *picture,* ⟍ *spider,* ⟋ *scatter.*

55

Circle S is added to half-length strokes and to double-length strokes in the normal way, and is always read last: ‿ *fat*, ‿ *fats*, ╲‿ *feature*, ╲‿ *features*.

PRACTICE FORTY-THREE (Key on p. 141)
Read and copy several times

Note: Upward L standing alone is doubled for TR only, as in: ⌐ *latter*, ⌐ *letter*, ⌐ *litter*.

Short Forms

To be copied and memorized:

‿ *what*, ⊃ *would*, ⌣ *hand*, ⤙ *under*, ′ *ought/awe*, ↙ *who*, ╲ *put*,) *therefore*, ⋀ *respect/ed*.

Phrases

The Doubling Principle is used in phrases to represent the words *there*, *their*, and *dear*. Read and copy the following forms:

⟨ *I shall be there*, ⟨ *I think there is*, ⌢ *I know there is*, ⌣ *in their*, ⌣ *in their view*, ╲ *my dear sir*, ⌢ *my dear Smith*, ⌣ *for your letter*,

......✓...... *in your letter,* ......ᒻ......... *in this matter,* ³... *what you,*

₃ *would you,* ₃·· *would you be,* ᖇ·· *you would,* ⁓ *in hand,*

⤳ *under the,* ⟨ *ought to be,* .₆.. *who is/has,* ✓.... *who will,*

ℒ *those who are,* ⌒⌒ *let me know.*

PRACTICE FORTY-FOUR (Key on p. 141)
Read and copy several times

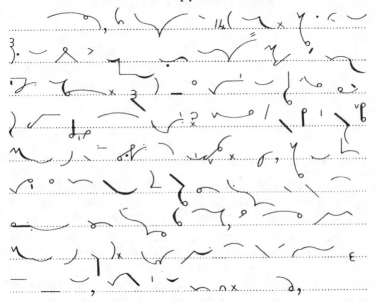

PRACTICE FORTY-FIVE (Key on p. 141)
Write in shorthand (from dictation if possible)

In the latter years of last century it was the habit for folk to put up so many pictures in their houses that few bare spaces could be seen. Copies of pictures— some good, some bad—could be made at little cost and sold for quite small sums of money. It was in the nature of things, therefore, that father should put up pictures all too solidly for the tastes of to-day. For to-day there is another vogue, a vogue for few pictures or for no pictures at all.

We view with small respect the masterpieces that hung in father's house and if, by bad luck, any of them come into our hands, we cast them away if possible or hide them in the attic; but in the future tastes may alter, may swing back, and attics may be searched for the pictures and masterpieces despised by us to-day.

FACILITY DRILL ELEVEN

(a)
(b)
(c)
(d)

Dictation Test Seven

It is possible that after some practice you will be able to write these 100 words from dictation in two minutes. Check your notes from the shorthand Key on p. 142.

Sirs, I wish to order another dozen copies of the[10] book *Some Nature Studies* by Harry Anderson. This book has[20] a ready sale with the public as well as being[30] a very good handbook for those who are making a[40] special study of such matters. It would be of service[50] to me if in future you would send me copies[60] of your book list early in each month so that[70] I can let you have my order in good time.[80] The Saunders book *Letters from Father* is not selling, and[90] I think I shall have copies left on hand. Yours,[100]

LESSON TWELVE

Stroke L

The curve for L can be as conveniently written downwards as upwards, and advantage is taken of this fact to provide easily written outlines and also for purposes of vowel indication.

You already know that L is written downwards when halved for D, as in ⟍ *fold,* ⟍ *field.* If you will read and copy the following outlines you will see a further use of the downward L:

only, until, kneel, wrongly

natural, naturally, unnatural

recent, recently

centre, central, centrally

facile, nicely, pencil

lesson, lessons, listen

In these outlines the L is written downwards in order to give easily written forms. It is written downwards (1) after ⟍ N and ⟍ NG, and (2) before and after a left-motion circle and curve, in order to maintain the direction of writing. Compare ⟍ *lesson,* ⟋ *vessel,* ⟍ *pencil,* in which a left motion of writing is maintained throughout, with ⟋ *muscle,* ⟋ *Leslie,* in which the curves and circle are written with the right motion throughout.

PRACTICE FORTY-SIX (Key on p. 142)
Read and copy several times

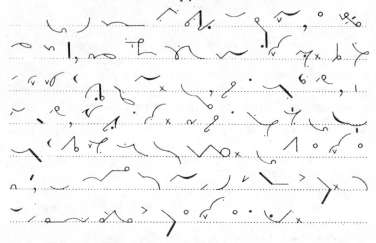

In the following outlines, stroke L is written downwards or upwards according to the presence or absence of a vowel:

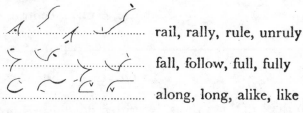

rail, rally, rule, unruly

fall, follow, full, fully

along, long, alike, like

The rule that governs the writing of the above outlines is: (1) After straight upstrokes and after F, V, SK write final L downwards if there is no final vowel and upwards if a vowel follows the L. In speed writing, therefore, the use of the Upward L indicates the presence of the vowel and there is no need to insert it. (2) Write L downwards initially before horizontal strokes when there is an initial vowel and upwards if there is no vowel. Again, the fact that the initial L is written downwards indicates the presence of a vowel and there is no need in speed writing actually to show it.

Short Forms

To be copied and memorized:

⌐ *oh/owe*, ⌐ *influence*, ⌐ *Lord*, ⌐ *whatever*,
⌐ *whenever*, ⌐ *electric*, ⌐ *electricity*, ⌐ *regular*,
⌐ *irregular*.

Phrases

Read and copy:

⌐ *as a matter of fact*, ⌐ *in this respect*, ⌐ *I feel*,
⌐ *I could not*, ⌐ *in all matters*, ⌐ *in his*, ⌐
in future.

PRACTICE FORTY-SEVEN (Key on p. 142)
Read and copy several times

PRACTICE FORTY-EIGHT (Key on p. 143)
Write in shorthand (from dictation if possible)

Since I have had electricity put into my house I have made regular use of my electric fires and cooking apparatus and utensils. I got along nicely with the oil stove when it was necessary for me to use it, but I feel that it is very satisfactory and much faster to cook by electricity. As a matter of fact, I feel that I can rely on the results in a way I could not with the oil stove. I may alter my views in this respect, but I doubt it. You and I are alike in the desire to be up-to-date in all matters relating to the house, and to do whatever we can to reduce dirt and dust. Naturally, I make full use of my electric vacuum whenever I can.

Dictation Test Eight (Key on p. 143)

Try to write the following 120 words in two minutes. If at first this is too fast for you, take the piece down in separate half-minutes, and then try the whole passage.

Lord Slaughter, in his capacity as head of the Central[10] Electric Undertaking, said:

"I can honestly say that much of[20] the success I have reported to you is due to[30] the loyalty of our staff, and we owe them a[40] debt of thanks. Sometimes I think that the influence of[50] the staff is not fully understood and I like to[60] do whatever I can, whenever I can, to indicate our[70] thanks in a fitting way. Your Board has therefore, influenced[80] by my wishes, decided to give the staff a bonus[90] this year of a month's pay. If our results are[100] as satisfactory in future years as in the past year[110] or two this staff bonus may be a regular feature."[120]

LESSON THIRTEEN

Diphones

A small angular sign, representing two consecutively sounded vowels, is called a Diphone and its use is illustrated in the following outlines:

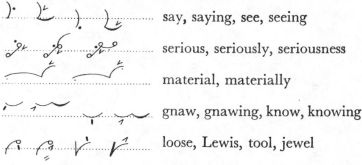

say, saying, see, seeing

serious, seriously, seriousness

material, materially

gnaw, gnawing, know, knowing

loose, Lewis, tool, jewel

A study of these outlines should teach you two things, the first that the angular sign for the Diphone _ᴗ_ or _ᴖ_ is written in the position of the first of the two vowels; and the second that the sign opens towards the right when the first of the vowels would normally be represented by a dot, and to the left when the first vowel would normally be represented by a dash. Compare _ᴗ_ *saying* with _ᴗ_ *sewing;* _ᴗ_ *really* with _ᴖ_ *ruin.*

The sign _ᴗ_ is also used to represent the consecutive vowels heard in the last syllable of such words as: _ᴗ_ *righteous,* _ᴗ_ *digestion,* _ᴗ_ *suggestion.*

You are already familiar with the Triphone, as used in the outlines: _ᴗ_ *dial,* _ᴗ_ *boyish,* _ᴗ_ *power,* _ᴗ_ *fewer.*

63

PRACTICE FORTY-NINE (Key on p. 144)
Read and copy several times

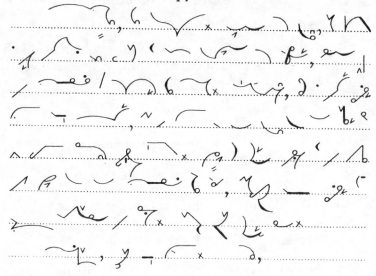

Consonant H

H is one of the consonants for which additional signs are given so that the shorthand writer is able to write legible and speedy outlines in all cases. The upward form of HAY ⌒ is generally used, as: ⌒ *hope,* ⌒ *happy,* ⌒ *Harry,* ⌒ *head.*

Downward H

The downward form ⌇ is used in the following outlines:

				high, higher, highest, highly
				he, hike, hiking, Hague
				cohere, mahogany, Lahore

This downward form is used: (1) when HAY stands alone, and in derivatives of such outlines; (2) before ____ K and ____ G; and (3) after horizontal strokes and L.

Note: The Short Form _ᴧ_ *he* is used only when joined to a preceding stroke, as in: ⸜ *that he.* In other cases the stroke form _⸝_ is used, as in: _⸝_ *he is,* _⸝_ *he can.*

Tick H

The downward H is reduced to a little tick before ⌒ **M,** ⌐ **Upward L,** and ⌒. **Downward R,** as shown in the outlines:

↳ ⌐ ⼨ ⼨ home, whole, hold, holding

⌐ ⌐ ⼰ ⸝ her, hear, hurt, hard

The word *HoMeLieR* is a useful memory aid for the use of Tick H.

In a few outlines the stroke for H is omitted, the Aspirate being either omitted from the outline or indicated by a dot, as in: ⤳ *uphill,* ⼅ *leasehold,* ⼝ *sweetheart.*

PRACTICE FIFTY (Key on p. 144)
Read and copy several times

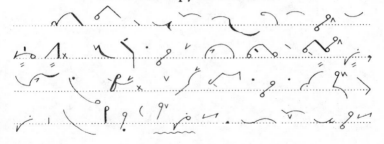

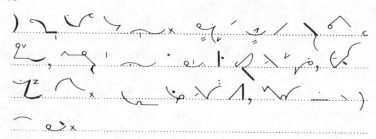

Short Forms

To be copied and memorized:

yard, word, myself, himself, itself, because, several, interest, interested.

Phrases

Read and copy:

so much, very much, too much, how much, in here, for her, to hear, I have heard, for several, for several years, we are interested.

You will see that in the first four phrases the outline for *much* is written in full in order to give useful phrases for common expressions.

PRACTICE FIFTY-ONE (Key on p. 144)
Read and copy several times

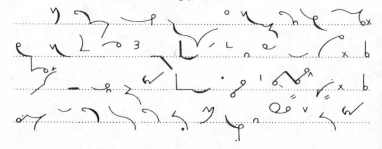

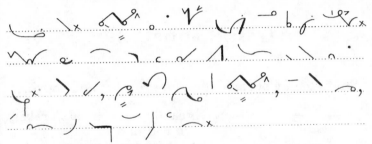

PRACTICE FIFTY-TWO (Key on p. 145)

Write in shorthand (from dictation if possible)

Miss R. Mayers,
Castle House,
East Hills.

My dear Madam, We thank you for your order for
21 yards of the pink silk material at £1·50 per yard.
Our buyer, Miss Hicks, is herself seeing to the dispatch
of this material, and I think I am safe in saying that it
will reach you by next Tuesday or earlier.

In November we are holding a show of some very
lovely Chinese silks, and we think you would be very
much interested in seeing these materials if you can
spare the time to come along. The showing is for
buyers only, and is to be held from the 4th to the 14th of
the month. Yours,

FACILITY DRILL TWELVE

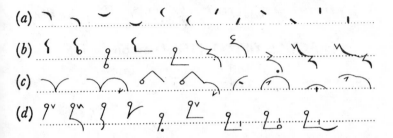

LESSON FOURTEEN

Hook R

Study the following outlines by reading and copying:

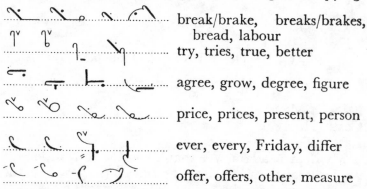

break/brake, breaks/brakes, bread, labour

try, tries, true, better

agree, grow, degree, figure

price, prices, present, person

ever, every, Friday, differ

offer, offers, other, measure

In these outlines a small initial hook has been used for R, a consonant that is often used in combination with another consonant. The Hook R is written (1) with the right motion to straight strokes (that is, on the side opposite to the Circle S); and (2) inside curves.

Hook R is used (1) when R immediately follows another consonant, as in: ⏧ *DRess,* ⏤ *CRedit,* ⏤ *FRiday;* and (2) for such syllables as TER, DER, FER, ZHER, etc., as in: ⏤ *OctoBER,* ⏤ *waTER,* ⏤ *eiTHER,* ⏤ *meaSURE,* ⏤ *diFFER,* ⏤ *PERhaps.*

PRACTICE FIFTY-THREE (Key on p. 145)
Read and copy several times

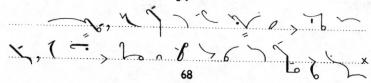

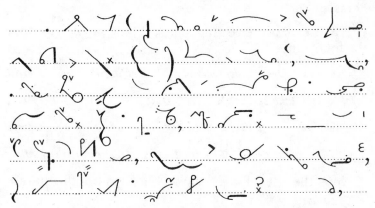

Note: The hooked forms are not usually used in words of one syllable. The very common words *girl* and *term* are, however, written with the hooked forms, as: ⌒, ↆ×. Compare ↆ *terse,* ⤳ *firm,* where the full forms are used.

Short Forms

To be copied and memorized:

⟋ *ourselves,* ⟆ *themselves,* ⟋ *rather/writer,* ⟋ *doctor,*
⟋ *dear,* ⟋ *during,* ⌐ *guard,* ⌐ *great,* ⌐ *care,*
⌒ *immediate,* ⌒ *immediately.*

Intersections

Rapid phrases are obtained by striking one consonant stroke, representing an often used word, through another stroke. Stroke P, for instance, may be intersected to represent *party* and stroke B to represent *bank* or *bill,* as in the phrases:

⤬ *birthday party,* ⟆ *this party,* ⤳ *in your party;*
⟆ *this bank,* ⤬ *to our bank,* ⤳ *new bill,* ⤬ *insurance bill.*

Phrases

Practise the intersecting phrases illustrated, and also the following:

⟍ *dear sir,* ⟍ *dear madam,* ⟍ *during the,* ⟍ *great care,* ⟍ *take care,* ⟍ *very truly,* ⟍ *very truly yours,* ⟍ *in our,* ⟍ *in our time,* ⟍ *in our view,* ⟍ *every day,* ⟍ *great deal,* ⟍ *I trust,* ⟍ *about the matter.*

Note the use of the Hook R for *our* in the phrase ⟍ *in our.*

PRACTICE FIFTY-FOUR (Key on p. 146)

Read and copy several times

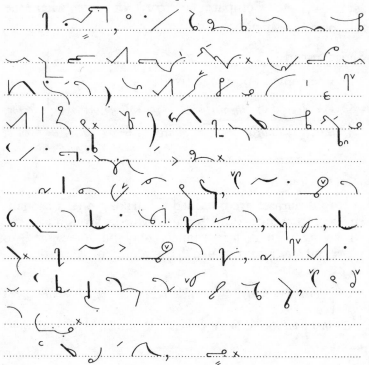

PRACTICE FIFTY-FIVE (Key on p. 146)

Write in shorthand (from dictation if possible)

Doctor Jeffrey states that we should immediately take this new[10] bill across to our bank and ask them if they[20] think it is to be paid by ourselves or some[30] other party.

As a matter of fact, we feel that[40] this bill should never have come to us, and we[50] rather differ from the doctor in that we think it[60] should be sent back to the builders immediately. As they[70] themselves admit, the property has not needed a great deal[80] of repair during the time that we have occupied these[90] premises, and we are certainly not prepared to pay for[100] anything carried out prior to our moving in.

Still, we[110] must act carefully, and perhaps it would be better for[120] you to get into touch with the firm who previously[130] occupied the premises and ask them what they themselves think[140] about the matter.   (143 words)

Dictation Test Nine

Try to write Practice Fifty-five within three minutes, and then within two minutes.

LESSON FIFTEEN

Circles and Loops Combined with Hook R

Read and copy the following outlines, studying them carefully:

soap, set, stoke

spray, stray, screw

supper, stutter, stoker

sweeper, sweeter, swagger

In these outlines the Circle or Loop incorporates the R Hook, and you are introduced for the first time to Circles and Loops written with the right motion when added to straight strokes. The fact that the Circle or Loop is written on the R Hook side of the stroke is an indication that the sound of R is included. Compare

soap with supper, and set with stray.

The Circle or Loop is written with this right motion (opposite to the normal motion): (1) when the consonants occur together, as in: SPRay, STRoll, SCReam; or (2) when a vowel separates the S, ST, or SW from the hooked form, as in: SuPPER, SToKER, SWeeTER.

Compare stay and set with stray and setter. Note also swag, swagger, and scheme, scream.

PRACTICE FIFTY-SIX (Key on p. 147)

Read and copy several times

[shorthand outlines]

In the case of Circle S occurring in combination with Hook R added to curves, both Circle and Hook are shown, and this applies also in the middle of an outline. The following outlines illustrate this:

[shorthand]   sum, safe, soon

[shorthand]   summer, safer, sooner

[shorthand]   industry, express, distribute

Note, however, such outlines as *[shorthand]* *disagree,* *[shorthand]* *discourse,* where it is not practicable to show both Circle and Hook.

NG-GR/KR

There are two forms for this combination of consonants —the Hooked form ◡ or the Double-length form ⌒.

The Double-length form is most conveniently used when it is the first stroke consonant in an outline and after upstrokes, as: ⌒ *anger,* ◡ *sinker,* ⌒ *longer;* but ◡ *finger,* ◡ *banker,* ⌐ *drinker.*

Note the use of the Downward R after NG to represent the final syllable heard in ◡ *singer,* ⌒ *hanger.* Compare ◡ *singer* with ◡ *sinker,* and ⌒ *hanger* with ⌒ *hanker.*

Stroke L

You will remember from Lesson Eleven that Stroke L standing alone is doubled only for the addition of TR. Note, therefore, the use of the hooked form in ⌐ *ladder,* ⌐ *leader.*

Short Forms

To be copied and memorized:

⌒ *particular,* ⌒ *opportunity,* ⌐ *tried,* ⌐ *trade/toward,* ⌒ *character,* ⌒ *characteristic,* ⟍ *probable/probably/probability,* ⟍ *improbable,* ⌒ *everything.*

Phrases

Read and copy:

⟍ *in all probability,* ⟍ *to us,* ◡ *for us,* ⌒ *let us,* ⌐ *let us see,* ⌐ *let us have,* ◡ *let us know,* ⟍ *your attention,* ◡ *particular attention,* ⊣ *to give attention,* ◡ *yours truly.*

Note the use of Circle S for *us* and of the intersected stroke T for *attention.*

PRACTICE FIFTY-SEVEN (Key on p. 147)

Read and copy several times

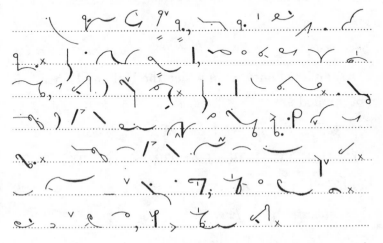

PRACTICE FIFTY-EIGHT (Key on p. 147)

Write in shorthand (from dictation if possible)

Dear Strong, This is to report to you that, as you thought probable, the speaker who summed up the debate expressed the view that our industry would prosper better if we could get some satisfactory method by which to distribute our products. He laid particular stress on the necessity in a trade of this character for the regular dispatch of goods, and he tried to make useful suggestions, some of which could be of real help to us. I paid particular attention to what he said, and in all probability I shall draw up a full scheme with proposals for operating on a different basis in future. I hope to see you soon. Yours truly,

REVISION THREE

In the course of Lessons Ten to Fifteen the following principles have been dealt with:

HALVING FOR T AND D, as illustrated in the outlines: *notes*, *late*, *part*, *starts*, *goods*, *relating*, *rapidly*, *rabbits*, *end*, *made*, *field*, *feared*, *wanted*, *ended*.

Examples of outlines in which the Halving Principle is not applied are: *minute*, *fact*, *rate*, *paid*, *bat*, *carried*, *followed*.

DOUBLING FOR TR, DR, THR, TURE, as illustrated in the outlines: *letters*, *material*, *father*, *future*, *operator*, *anger*, *longer*, *hunger*.

Examples of outlines in which the Doubling Principle is not employed are: *ladder*, *Peter*, *cater*.

DOWNWARD L as used in: *only*, *until*, *natural*, *honestly*, *lesson*, *railings*, *fall*, *along*, *scale*.

DOWNWARD H as used in: *high*, *higher*.

TICK H as used in: *home*, *her*, *hills*.

DOT H as used in: *perhaps*, *leasehold*.

DIPHONES as used in: *saying*, *seeing*, *knowing*, *Lewis*, *suggestions*.

HOOK R as illustrated in the outlines: try, better, labour, prices, offers, other, measure, bankers, sober, sweeter, stutter, expresses, industrial, summer, safer.

Short Forms

(This list to be used as a Facility Drill)

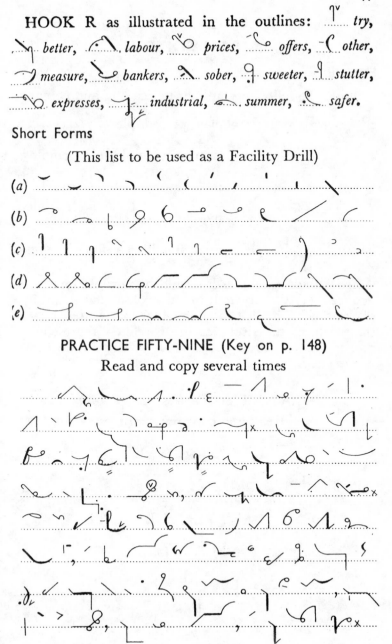

(a)

(b)

(c)

(d)

(e)

PRACTICE FIFTY-NINE (Key on p. 148)

Read and copy several times

LESSON SIXTEEN

Hook L

Study the following outlines by reading and copying:

play, played, place, places

employ, employed, employs, employers

table, tables, trouble, troubles

fly, flies, flight, flew/flue

final, finally, develop, developed

From these examples it should be possible for you to deduce: (1) that a small initial hook added to straight strokes with the left motion—that is, written on the same side of the stroke as the Circle S—represents *L;* and (2) that a large initial hook written inside curves represents *L.*

PRACTICE SIXTY (Key on p. 148)

Read and copy several times

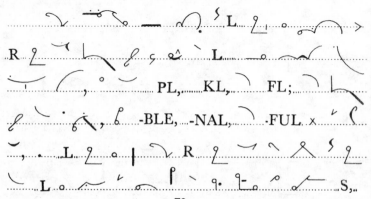

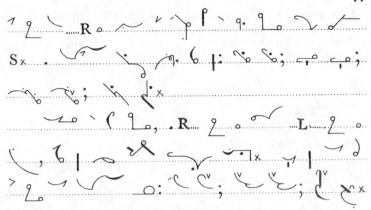

Circle S Combined with Hook L

Circle S may be written inside the L Hook so that both Circle and Hook are clearly shown. Read and copy the following outlines:

splash, splashes, split, splits

supply, supplies, possible, possibly

person, personal, personally

As these outlines illustrate, the Circle S is combined with Hook L: (1) when the consonants occur together, as in: *SPLash;* or (2) when a vowel separates the S from the hooked form, as in: *SuPPLy*, *perSoNAL.*

Vocalization of Hooked Forms

It sometimes happens that a more rapid or more easily written outline for a common word can be obtained by using the hooked forms—or Double Consonants, as they are also called—even though an accented vowel occurs between the consonant and the R or L. In such cases the vowel may be indicated by writing: (1) a dash vowel or a diphthong through the Double Consonant, as in: ⌒ *north,* ⌐ *record,* ⌐ *political,* ⌐ *further,* ⌐ *lecture;* and (2) a small circle in the place of a dot vowel, as in: ⌐ *garden,* ⌐ *regard,* ⌐ *engineer,* ⌐ *direct.*

These hooked forms are not generally used in words of one syllable, which are written with the separate consonants, as in: ⌐ *pale,* ⌐ *pair,* ⌐ *poll,* ⌐ *poor.* In a very few common words, however, the hooked form is used, as: ⌐ *coarse/course,* ⌐ *nurse.*

Note the special distinguishing outlines: ⌐ *regard,* ⌐ *regret.*

Short Forms

To be copied and memorized:

⌐ *belief/believe/d,* ⌐ *build/ing,* ⌐ *call,* ⌐ *called,* ⌐ *equal/ly,* ⌐ *tell,* ⌐ *told,* ⌐ *till,* ⌐ *electrical,* ⌐ *represent/ed.*

Phrases

Read and copy:

⌐ *I am pleased,* ⌐ *it is clear,* ⌐ *not only,* ⌐ *of course,* ⌐ *in the course,* ⌐ *I am able to,* ⌐ *we are unable to,* ⌐ *by all,* ⌐ *at all,* ⌐ *first-class.*

PRACTICE SIXTY-ONE (Key on p. 148)
Read and copy several times

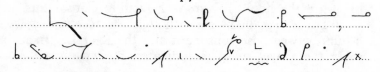

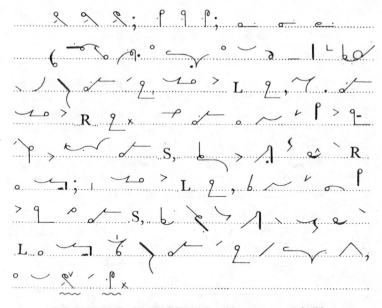

PRACTICE SIXTY-TWO (Key on p. 149)
Write in shorthand (from dictation if possible)

Dear Miss Black, I must express my thanks to you[10] for your letter and for the beautiful drawings in blue[20] chalk.

I personally believe these drawings to be first-class,[30] and I shall submit them to my Board of Directors[40] at the first opportunity. I think the drawings are likely[50] to meet with equal approval from my colleagues, but till[60] they have seen them I am, of course, unable to[70] make you an offer for their purchase. I hope to[80] be able to write to you further on this matter[90] in the course of the next few days.

I should[100] be very pleased to see you and discuss the whole[110] matter with you if you can call in here at[120] any time. Yours faithfully, (124 words)

LESSON SEVENTEEN

Reverse Forms for FR, FL, etc.

R and L are among the most frequently used consonants in the English language, and because of this the Pitman system makes the maximum use of the R and L Hooks. You have already learned: (1) that a small initial Hook to straight strokes adds L when written with the Left Motion and R when written with the Right Motion; and (2) that a small initial Hook written inside curves adds R and a large Hook adds L.

In this Lesson you will see that certain of these hooked curves are turned over, or reversed, to provide alternative forms. Study carefully the following pairs:

fr	vr	thr	THr	fl	vl

The first form of each pair is called the Left form and is written with the Left Motion, and the second is called the Right form and is written with the Right Motion.

The following outlines illustrate the use of these alternative, or reverse, forms, and you are advised to study them very carefully by reading and copying:

(a) fry, free, through, three

(b) Africa, frame, cover, leather

(c) rifle, novel, cavil, gravely

The Reverse, or Right, form of FR, VR, thR, THR is used:

(1) *For Purposes of Vowel Indication* when the hooked form stands by itself, and has no vowel before it, as illustrated under (a) above. Note the following contrasting pairs: *offer,* *free;* *ether,* *three.* If no

vowel were inserted in such outlines, you would know whether the vowel occurred before or after the consonants.

(2) *For Purposes of Facility in Writing* when a more easily written outline results. Generally, it is better to join the right forms to strokes written towards the right, as illustrated under (*b*). Note the contrasting outlines:

Friday, *verge,* but *verb,* *freak,* *river.*

The Right form of thR is generally used, as in *thirty,* *Thursday,* *thirsty,* *thread.*

The Reverse or Right form of FL/VL is used after a straight upstroke or the horizontal strokes — K, — G, and ⏝ N, as illustrated under (*c*) and by the outlines:

roughly, *hovel,* *naval.* In other cases the Left form is used, as in: *flow,* *aflow,* *flame,* *joyful,* *arrival.*

PRACTICE SIXTY-THREE (Key on p. 149)
Read and copy several times

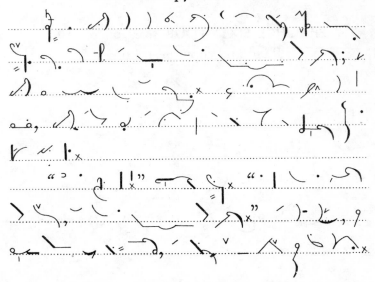

84

Short Forms

To be copied and memorized:

⌠ *deliver/ed/delivery,* ⌇ *people,* ⌢ *cold/equalled,* ⌢
gold, ⌢⌣ *golden,* ⌒ *short,* ⌒ *shorthand,* ⌒ *pleasure,*
⌢ *more/remark/ed,* ⌢ *Mr./mere,* ⌢ *merely,* ⟍
member/remember/ed, ⟍ *number/ed.*

Phrases

Read and copy:

⌇ *very short,* ⟍ *I have pleasure,* ⌢ *we have the*
pleasure, ⌢ *Mr. Smith,* ⌿ *on Thursday last,* ⌢ *from*
their/there, ⌢ *more and more,* ⌢ *more or less,* ⟋ *your*
company, ⌿ *this company,* ⟊ *in charge,* ⟋ *free of*
charge, ⌿ *yours faithfully.*

Note the use of the intersected K for *company* and CH
for *charge/ed.*

PRACTICE SIXTY-FOUR (Key on p. 150)
Read and copy several times

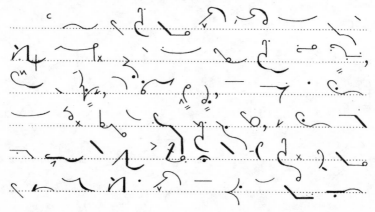

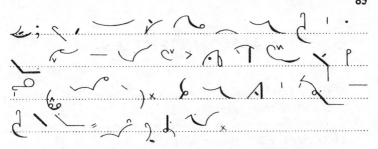

PRACTICE SIXTY-FIVE (Key on p. 150)
Write in shorthand (from dictation if possible)

Did you write any shorthand on Thursday and are
you going to write any shorthand on Friday? It is
hoped that your zeal for writing shorthand is equalled
only by your love for reading it. When reading you
should pay close attention to the phrasing used, and when
writing you should try to develop an easy and flowing
style. It is very probable that with every Lesson you
grow more and more fascinated by these beautiful
little signs, and get more pleasure from their use. A
knowledge of shorthand has brought golden opportunities
to very many people, and an ability to write the shorthand characters rapidly is of benefit to all who possess it.

LESSON EIGHTEEN

Hook N

A small final hook, written (1) with the Right Motion when added to straight strokes, and (2) inside curves, represents the sound of N. Note carefully the use of the N Hook in the following outlines:

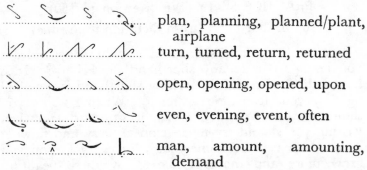

plan, planning, planned/plant, airplane

turn, turned, return, returned

open, opening, opened, upon

even, evening, event, often

man, amount, amounting, demand

From these outlines you will see that a stroke that is hooked for N may be halved in length to add either T or D, and this rule is further illustrated by the outlines: *paint/pained*, *lent/lend*, *spent/spend*, *friend*, *front*.

The word-ending NT or ND is generally represented by combining the use of the N Hook with the Halving Principle.

PRACTICE SIXTY-SIX (Key on p. 150)
Read and copy several times

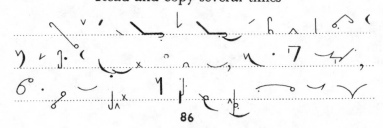

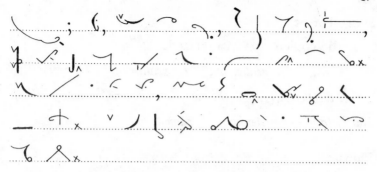

Circle or Loop Combined with Hook N

Circle S following Hook N to curves is written inside the hook so that both circle and hook are clearly shown, as in: events, demands, fans.

A Circle or Loop following Hook N to straight strokes is written with the Right Motion, that is, on the N Hook side of the stroke, as in: dance, dances, danced, Dunster, plans, engines, once, distance. The fact that this Circle or Loop is written on the side opposite to the normal Circle or Loop is an indication that the sound of N is included.

The two outlines train and strains provide valuable memory-aids to the correct use of the Right Motion Hooks and Circles.

When the light sound of NS follows a curve, the stroke N is used in order to allow for derivative outlines, as in: fence, fenced, fences; annoyance, annoyances. Compare the use of the Hook N and Circle to represent the heavy sound of NZ, in the outlines: Fens, vans, where the question of derivatives does not arise.

Short Forms

To be copied and memorized:

⟍ *been*,   ⌣ *gentleman*,   ⌣ *gentlemen*,   ∫ *general/ly*,

↗ *wonderful/ly*,   ⟍ *become*,   ⌐ *income*,   ⟍ *practice/*

practise/d,   ⌁ *yesterday*,   ⌐ *cannot*.

Phrases

Read and copy:

⌐ *again and again*,   ⌣ *ladies and gentlemen*,   ⌐ *at the moment*,   ∫ *in general*,   ⌁ *of yesterday*,   ⟍ *has been*, ⟍ *I have been*,   ⌁ *we had been*,   ⟍ *I have been there*, ∫ *I do not*,   ⟍ *I did not know*,   ⌐ *I will not*, ⌒ *you are not*,   ⟍ *better than*,   ⌁ *higher than*,   ⌐ *I cannot*.

Note the use of the N Hook in phrasing to represent the words *been* and *than*, and its combination with the Halving Principle for the representation of *not*. This class of phrase is particularly useful, and the principle should be applied whenever practicable.

PRACTICE SIXTY-SEVEN (Key on p. 151)
Read and copy several times

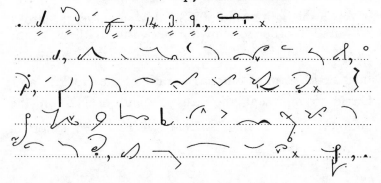

PRACTICE SIXTY-EIGHT (Key on p. 151)
Write in shorthand (from dictation if possible)

Again and again you have read, under *Practice*, the words "Read and copy several times." This advice is helpful because by reading you become so used to seeing the various shorthand outlines that, when you take notes, the correct outlines leap into your mind without your having to think about rules. Your mind, as a matter of fact, becomes a store-room for pictures of outlines. The more pictures of outlines you have stored away in your mind, for automatic use when needed, the better and faster is your writing likely to be.

By writing you become used to forming the outlines with facility and in such a manner that you can depend upon your notes and can easily read back what has been written.

Have you tried yet to write at one hundred words a minute? Perhaps you have not, but it is possible that you can already write at this speed. In *Practice* 67 there are one hundred words. Turn to the Key, which is counted in ten's, and if possible have this read out to you, not once only but several times, and see if you can write the first fifty words in thirty seconds. Then try to write the one hundred words in one minute. One day you may have the wonderful and thrilling experience of writing at two hundred words a minute.

If you want to reach higher and still higher speeds, then read and copy, learn the rules, do plenty of note-taking, and plenty of facility practice.

LESSON NINETEEN

Hook F and V

From a study of the following outlines you will see that a small hook, written with a Left Motion at the end of a straight stroke, adds the sound of either F or V:

drive, drives, driving, drove

serve, serves, served, half

profit, profits, provide, provides

The F/V Hook is added to straight strokes only, and there is no corresponding hook to curves, the stroke F or V being used, as in the outlines: *muff*, *mauve*, *loaf*, *loaves*, *arrive*, *orphans.*

The Circle S is written inside the F/V Hook so that both Circle and Hook are clearly shown, as in: *chiefs*, *caves.*

A stroke hooked for F or V may be halved for either T or D, as in: *puffed*, *paved*, *draft*, *halved.*

Short Forms

To be copied and memorized:

nor, *northern*, *near*, *over*, *however*, *principal/principle*, *liberty*, *opinion*, *together*, *altogether*, *commercial/ly*, *southern.*

90

Phrases

Read and copy:

⌒ *in our opinion,* ⌒ *in their opinion,* ⌒ *in my opinion,* ⌐ *over the,* ⌒ *nearer than,* ⌐ *together with,*) *they are,*) *they are not,* / *which have,* / *which have been,* / *who have not,* [*set of,* | *out of,* ⟨ *Labour Government,* ⟩ *in the form,* ⟩ *new forms.*

In these phrases the R Hook to curves has been used to represent the word *are,* the F/V Hook to represent the words *have* and *of;* an intersected ⎯ GAY has been used for *Government* and an intersected ⟍ F for *form.* In the case of intersected strokes, the phrases given are intended as examples only, and full use should be made of the principle of intersection.

PRACTICE SIXTY-NINE (Key on p. 152)

Read and copy several times

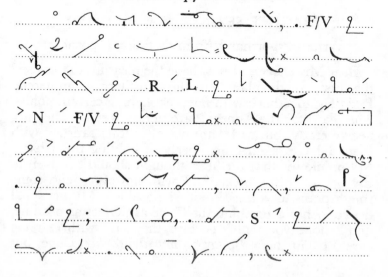

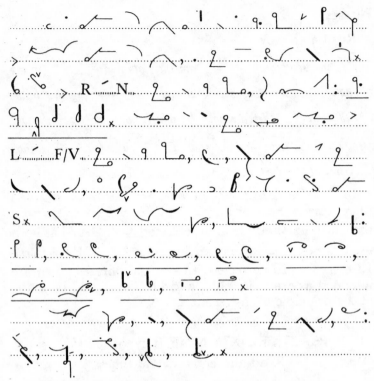

PRACTICE SEVENTY (Key on p. 153)

Write in shorthand (from dictation if possible)

Dear Mr. Driver, I now have the pleasure to enclose[10] the first rough plans for the Northern Commercial Building, together[20] with notes explaining certain points. The plans for the Annexe[30] are not enclosed. They are nearly ready, but as I[40] am not altogether satisfied with them I have taken the[50] liberty of holding them back. My opinion is that further[60] thought should be given to the size of this Annexe.[70] I will, however, send some rough plans to you as[80] soon as possible. My principal desire is that everything shall[90] be as perfect as possible, and I hope you will[100] go over the plans with extreme care. I lent these[110] plans to my friend, Mr. Dove, but he returned them,[120] saying that he had neither the time nor the detailed[130] knowledge to be of service.

With kind regards and trusting[140] you will find the plans satisfactory,

I am,

Yours faithfully,[150]

FACILITY DRILL THIRTEEN

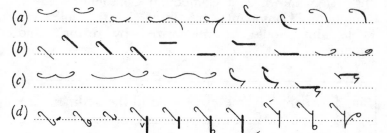

LESSON TWENTY

Compound Consonants

Certain combinations of consonants occur with great frequency in the English language, and in Pitmans Shorthand these combinations are represented by a single sign known as a Compound Consonant. These Compound Consonants are listed in the following Table and should be memorized by reading and copying.

Sign	Letter	Name	As in the outlines	
⌣	QU	kway	quick,	require
⌣	GU	gway	Gwynne,	sanguine
⌢	MP/MB	imp/imb	jump,	bamboo
⌒	LR	ler	fuller,	ruler
⌐	RR	rer	poorer,	clearer
⌿	WH	whay	white,	whisk
⌒	WL	wel	well,	wills
⌒	WHL	whel	while,	whilst

The following points should be noted:

MP/MB

(1) The hooked forms ⌇⌇⌇⌇ are used when the P or B comes immediately after M, as in ⌇ *employ,* ⌇ *simple,* ⌇ *embrace.* Note, however, the outlines ⌇ *impel,* ⌇ *embezzle,* where an accented vowel occurs between the M and the P or B.

(2) Initial Hook R may be added to ⌇, as in ⌇ *hamper,* ⌇ *camber.* ⌇ may also be doubled to add R, as in ⌇ *September,* ⌇ *temper.* The hooked form is used after upstrokes and ⌇ K; in other cases the double-length form is used.

(3) The thickened stroke ⌇ is not used when the P is very lightly sounded, as in ⌇ *attempt,* ⌇ *prompt.* Compare ⌇ *trumpet,* where the P is clearly sounded.

LR

The Compound Consonant ⌇ (written downwards) is used only in those cases where the downward L would normally be used. Compare ⌇ *fuller* with ⌇ *smaller,* and ⌇ *ruler* with ⌇ *retailer.*

WL, WHL

The signs ⌇, ⌇ are not used when a vowel comes before the W. Compare ⌇ *while* with ⌇ *awhile.*

KW

Circle S is written inside the hook, as in ⌇ *squall,* ⌇ *squally.*

PRACTICE SEVENTY-ONE (Key on p. 153)
Read and copy several times

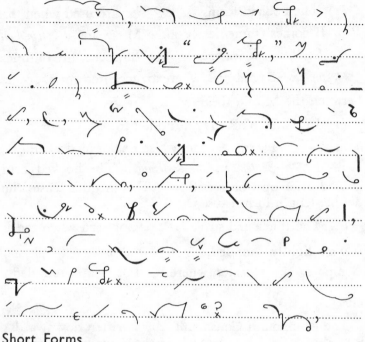

Short Forms

To be copied and memorized:

⁓ important/importance, ⁓ impossible, ⁓ improve/d/
improvement, ⌒ whether, ⁓ owing/language, ⌒ school,
⁓ surprise, ⌒ balance, ⌒ circumstance, ⁊ English,
⁊ England.

Phrases

Read and copy:

⌒ whether or not, ⁓ I am surprised, ⌒ in the circumstances, ⁓ in these circumstances, ⁓ in England,

.... *Bank of England*, ... *few months*, ... *next month*,
.... *this month*.

TH, intersected or joined, is used to represent the
word *month* in phrases.

PRACTICE SEVENTY-TWO (Key on p. 153)
Read and copy several times

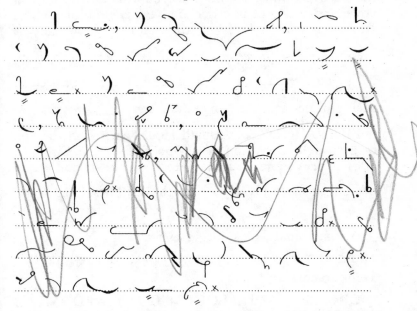

REVISION FOUR

In the course of Lessons Sixteen to Nineteen instruc-
tion has been mainly concentrated on the use of Initial
and Final Hooks. The following is a very brief summary
of what has been dealt with:

INITIAL HOOKS. A small Hook, written at the
beginning of a straight stroke on the same side as the
Circle S, adds L, and a similar Hook on the opposite

side of the stroke adds R, as in the outlines: ⟍. *play,* ⟍. *pray;* ⟍. *clay,* ⟍. *gray.*

A small initial Hook written inside curves adds R, and a large Hook adds L, as in the outlines: ⟍ *offer,* ⟍ *flow,* ⌐. *dinner,* ⌐. *tunnel.*

Certain initially hooked curves may be reversed or turned over to provide alternative forms for purposes of vowel indication or in order to give facile outlines. The Reverse Forms for FR, etc., are used in such outlines as: ⟍. *free,* ⟍. *frame,* ⟍. *Africa,* ⟍. *three,* ⟍. *river,* ⟍ *cover;* the Reverse Forms for FL, etc., are used in such outlines as: ⟍. *ruffle,* ⟍ *novel,* ⟍ *hovel.*

FINAL HOOKS. A small Hook, written at the end of a straight stroke on the same side as the Circle S, adds F or V, and a similar Hook on the opposite side of the stroke adds N, as in the outlines: ⌐. *tough,* ⌐. *ton;* ⟍. *cove,* ⟍. *cone.*

A small final Hook inside curves adds N, as in the outlines: ⟍. *fun,* ⟍. *thin,* ⟍. *earn.* There is no F/V Hook to curves.

CIRCLES AND LOOPS COMBINED WITH HOOKS. Generally, the Circle and Hook are both clearly shown, as in the outlines: ⌐. *settle,* ⟍. *sickle,* ⟍. *suffer,* ⟍. *civil,* ⌐. *disciple,* ⌐. *dishonour.*

A Circle or Loop written with the Right Motion, however, may include a Hook without the Hook being actually written, as in the outlines: ⌐. *setter,* ⌐. *stutter,* ⌐. *sweater;* ⌐ *dance,* ⌐ *dances,* ⌐ *danced,* ⌐. *Dunster.*

HOOKS ADDED TO COMPOUND CONSO-NANTS.

Final Hooks may be added to Compound Consonants in the same way as to simple consonants, as: ⌒ *queen,* ⌒ *hempen,* ⌒ *woollen.*

The Compound Consonant ⌒ MP/MB is hooked for R, as explained on p. 95 of this Lesson.

Short Forms

(This list to be used as a Facility Drill)

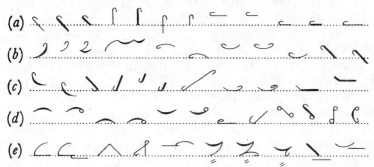

Phrases

Hooks are used in phrases to represent common words, as in: ⌠ *at all,* ⌡ *they are,* ⌣ *in our,* ⌐ *better than,* ⌐ *I have been,* ⌐ *out of,* ⌐ *who have.*

Dictation Test Ten

There are 229 words in the following Test. Try to take it down at the rate of 60 words a minute at the first attempt; then, after checking your shorthand from the Key on p. 154, take it down again, more than once, if possible, reaching a speed of at least 80 words a minute.

Your study of the rules up to this point will[10] have shown you that Pitmans Shorthand is built up upon[20] a very logical structure. There is, as you will have[30] realized, a sound purpose behind each rule; and each principle[40] is developed in a natural and brilliant way. Let us[50] for a moment analyse the building up of outlines from[60] the simple stroke with one vowel to the equally simple[70] sign that, while remaining quick and easy to write, represents[80] several sounds in one form. The following outlines illustrate this:[90] *pay, pays, space, sprays, sprains, sprained, sprint, sprinter, sprinters.*

The[100] first outline represents two sounds, the last outline represents nine[110] sounds; yet the last sign is almost as easily and[120] quickly written as the first.

A second set of outlines[130] of equal interest is: *pay, play, plays, splay, split, splint,[140] splints, splinter, splinters.*

It is owing to this logical development[150] of outlines through the use of Circles and Loops, and[160] through the varying length of strokes, that Pitmans Shorthand can[170] be written so quickly, and it is by no means[180] unusual for teachers to train writers up to speeds of[190] two hundred words a minute and over. Of course, it[200] requires practice to write at these high speeds, but there[210] is no question about the fact that it can be[220] done by those willing to do the necessary practice.   (229 words)

LESSON TWENTY-ONE

Shun Hook Added to Straight Strokes

Study the following outlines, reading and copying them several times:

action, actions, operation, operations

station, stations, exception, exceptional

distribution, distributions, perfection, perfections

You will see from these outlines that a large final hook is used to represent the very common syllable sounded SHUN, however spelt in longhand.

When added to straight strokes, the Shun Hook is written:

(1) FOR PURPOSES OF BALANCE on the side opposite to an initial Circle, Loop, or Hook, as in: *section*, *secretion*, *oppression*, *station;* and away from the curve when following ⟍⟋, whether light or heavy, as in: *affection*, *location*, *vacation*.

(2) FOR PURPOSES OF VOWEL INDICATION on the side of a plain straight stroke opposite to the last sounded vowel, as in: *action*, *caution*. Note: A vowel always occurs between T, D and J and the sound of SHUN, so that there is no need to use the principle of vowel indication in such cases, and the Shun Hook is written with the left motion, as in: *rotation*, *addition*, *magician*.

Circle S is written inside the Shun Hook so that both circle and hook are clearly shown.

S-Shun

The combination S-vowel-SHUN is represented by adding a little tail to the Circle, as in the outlines:

 decision, *position,* *transition,* *possession,* *accession.* A second-place vowel occurring between the S and SHUN is not shown; a third-place vowel is written at the side of the hook, as: *possession,* *position,* *decision,* *transition.*

PRACTICE SEVENTY-THREE (Key on p. 155)

Read and copy several times

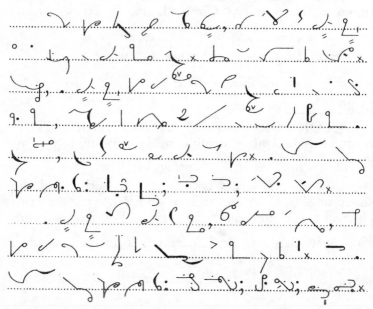

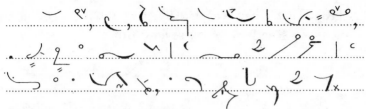

-Uation

The word-ending *-uation* is generally represented by the stroke SH and Hook N. Compare ⌡ *station* with ⌡ *situation*, and ⌐ *notation* with ⌐ *intuition*.

In the case of long words, where there is no possibility of confusion, however, the Shun Hook may be used, as in: ⌐ *perpetuation*, ⌐ *accentuation*.

Short Forms

To be copied and memorized:

⌐ *beyond*, ⌐ *subject/ed*, ⌐ *truth*, ⌐ *according*, ⌐ *object/ed*, ⌐ *objection*, ⌐ *representation*, ⌐ *satisfaction*, ⌐ *organize/d*, ⌐ *organization*, ⌐ *govern/ed*, ⌐ *Government*, ⌐ *advertise/d/ment*.

Phrases

Read and copy:

⌐ *according to*, ⌐ *according to the*, ⌐ *this morning*, ⌐ *to-morrow morning*, ⌐ *one million*, ⌐ *one thousand*, ⌐ *one hundred*, ⌐ *one hundred thousand*, ⌐ *one hundred million*, ⌐ £500, ⌐ £5,000, ⌐ £5,000,000.

Note the use of the intersected M for *morning*. Round numbers may be quickly represented, as shown above, by using M for *million*, TH for *thousand*, and N for *hundred*.

PRACTICE SEVENTY-FOUR (Key on p. 155)

Read and copy several times

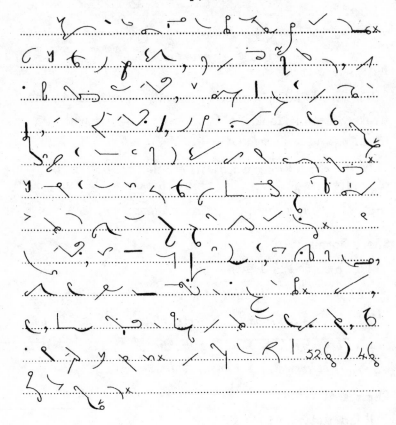

LESSON TWENTY-TWO

Shun Hook Added to Curves

From the following outlines you will see that the Hooks for SHUN and S-SHUN are used with curves, as well as with straight strokes:

nation, nations, attention, attentions

vision, visions, division, divisions

sense, senses, sensation, sensations

The SHUN Hook is, of course, written inside curves and, like other Hooks, it may be used in the middle of an outline, as in: *education*, *educational*, *nation*, *national*, *nationalization*, *transition*, *transitional*.

PRACTICE SEVENTY-FIVE (Key on p. 156)

Read and copy several times

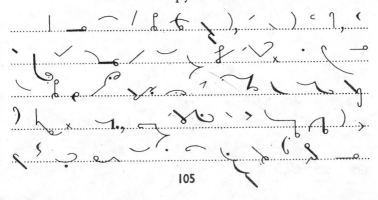

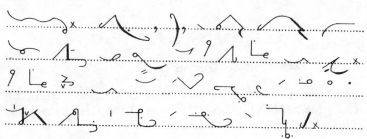

Upward SH

The Stroke SH ⟋ is as conveniently written upwards as downwards, and advantage is taken of this fact to provide more facile outlines in certain cases. Stroke SH is generally written upwards after *f* and *v*, as in ⟋ *fish*, ⟋ *vicious*, and also after *d*, as in ⎹ *dash*.

When following a straight stroke with an initial attachment, SH is generally written on the side opposite to such attachment, to preserve the balance of the outline. Note, for instance, the following outlines:

⟋ *blush* but ⟍ *brush;* ⟍ *splash* but ⎹ *trash.*

The general rule is that the downward form of SH is usually written, but the upward form may be used to obtain an easier joining, as in: ⟋ *sugar,* ⟍ *shackle,* ⟋ *shiver.*

SHR and SHL

The hooked form ⟋ SHR is always written downwards, and the hooked form ⟋ SHL is always written upwards, as in: ⟍ *fisher* but ⟍ *official,* ⟍ *pressure* but ⟍ *shilling.*

Short Forms

To be copied and memorized:

___ advantage, ___ own, ___ owner, ___ information, ___ influential/ly, ___ efficient/ly/cy, ___ sufficient/ly/cy, ___ deficient/ly/cy, ___ proficient/ly/cy, ___ investment, ___ sensible/ly/ility, ___ unanimous/ly/unanimity.

Phrases

Read and copy:

___ shorthand writer, ___ shorthand writing, ___ Pitmans Shorthand, ___ with regard to, ___ with regard to the, ___ in regard to, ___ in regard to the, ___ having regard to, ___ having regard to the, ___ national position, ___ national insurance, ___ national authorities, ___ Education Authority.

Note the use of the intersected N for *national* and TH for *authority*.

PRACTICE SEVENTY-SIX (Key on p. 156)
Read and copy several times

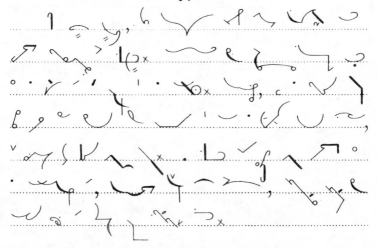

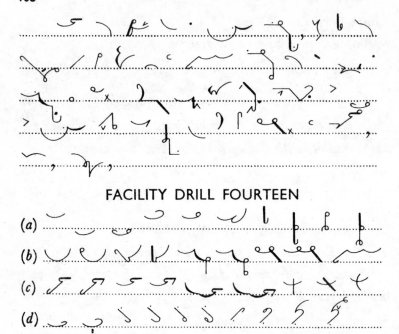

FACILITY DRILL FOURTEEN

(a)

(b)

(c)

(d)

LESSON TWENTY-THREE

Semicircle W

In the following outlines the consonant W is represented by a small semicircle:

walk, week/weak, walks, weeks/weaks

woman, women, women's, womanly

were, work, worth, worthy

quality, qualification, frequent, frequently

The semicircle W is used at the beginning of an outline when coming before ___ K, ___ G, ___ M, ___ Downward R and ___ Ray. It is not used if a vowel comes before the W, as illustrated in the following pairs of outlines: ___ *wake*, ___ *awake*; ___ *weary*, ___ *aweary*.

The semicircle W is sometimes used medially in order to provide a compact outline, as in: ___ *subsequent*, ___ *herewith*, ___ *twelve*, ___ *misquote*, ___ *Wordsworth*. You will see that, when used medially, the semicircle represents W plus a vowel, and that it is written in the position of the vowel. As with the Diphone sign, the semicircle W is open towards the right when including a dot vowel sign, as in ___ *farewell*, and towards the left when including a dash vowel sign, as in ___ *driftwood*.

* Note the distinguishing position of ___ *woman*.

PRACTICE SEVENTY-SEVEN (Key on p. 157)

Read and copy several times

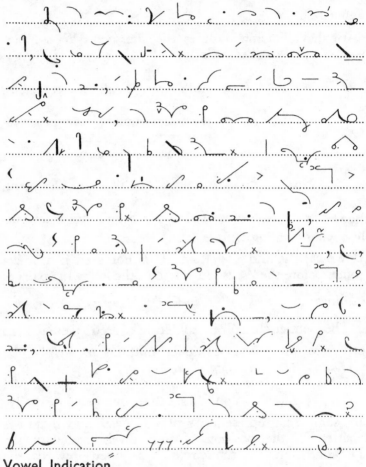

Vowel Indication

As you have already learned, the form of an outline can indicate the presence or absence of a vowel. This vowel indication is achieved principally by two means:

(1) *The use of an Upward or Downward form of Stroke*, as in: ⌒ *long*, but ⌒ *along*; ⌒ *lamb*, but ⌒ *elm*;

real, but *really;* *store*, but *story;* *rake*, but *ark;* and

(2) *The use or non-use of Circles, Loops, and Hooks,* as in: *sack*, but *ask;* *gas*, but *gassy;* *taste*, but *tasty;* *poster*, but *pastry;* *fun*, but *funny;* *puff*, but *puffy;* *pen*, but *penny;* *wake*, but *awake*, *while*, but *awhile.*

Where there is a vowel-sign there must be a stroke against which to place that sign. Therefore, the use of the stroke instead of the Circle, Loop, or Hook generally indicates that there is a vowel, and there is rarely any need to show the vowel-sign in the shorthand outline. For example, the final vowel is clearly indicated by the form of the outlines: illustrated above.

Stroke S

In addition to the use of Stroke S initially and finally for vowel indication purposes, the stroke form of S is used:

(1) Initially in outlines such as *size*, *cease*, *saucer*, where initial S is followed by a vowel and another S;

(2) At the beginning of an outline when followed by a triphone, as in: *science*, *scientific*, *suicide;*

(3) At the end of an outline when the final syllable *-ous* follows a diphthong, as *joyous*, *pious*.

-Sess

The final syllable *-sess* is generally written with the Circle S followed by a stroke, as in: ⟋ *possess,* ⟍ *access,* ⟍ *process.*

Short Forms

To be copied and memorized:

⟋ *child,* ⟍ *young,* ⟍ *younger,* ⟨ *within,* ⟩ *whose,* ⟩ *third,* ⟩ *sure,* ✝ *notwithstanding,* / *large,* ✝ *enlarge,* ⟍ *nevertheless,* ⟍ *inconvenience,* ⟋ *danger,* ⟋ *dangerous,* ⟋ *stranger,* ⟋ *messenger,* ⟋ *chair,* ⟋ *cheer,* ⟋ *cheered.*

Phrases

Read and copy:

⌒ *most important,* ⟍ *must be,* ⟍ *there must be,* ⟋ *last letter,* ⟍ *next week,* ⟍ *this week,* ⟍ *best possible,* ⟍ *least time,* ⟍ *I trust that.*

Note: In such phrases as ⌒ *most important,* ⟍ *must be,* and ⟋ *last letter,* a lightly-sounded consonant has been omitted. In phrases and in outlines a very lightly-sounded consonant may be omitted, as in: ⟋ *honestly,* ⟍ *postman,* ⟍ *mistake,* ⟍ *mistaken,* ⟍ *institute,* ⟍ *attempt,* ⟍ *prompt,* ⟍ *extinction.*

PRACTICE SEVENTY-EIGHT (Key on p. 157)
Read and copy several times

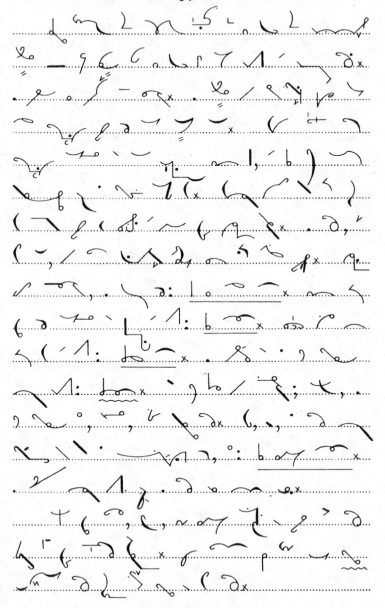

PRACTICE SEVENTY-NINE (Key on p. 158)

Write in shorthand (from dictation if possible)

I watched the children as they walked towards me. One child, whose hair was fair and curly, looked younger than the rest. It seemed to me that she was less joyous, less sure of herself, than the others. I noticed that she was, nevertheless, walking quickly in the attempt to keep up with the others. When they reached me I offered her 5p, but she shook her fair curls in a funny little way, and refused to take the 5p. I supposed she had been warned of the danger of talking to strangers. I watched them awhile, and then returned to the house, and forgot all about them. About half an hour later a messenger cycled up to my gate, and dismounted.

FACILITY DRILL FIFTEEN

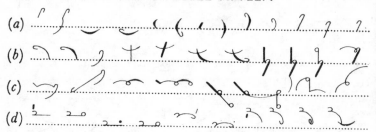

LESSON TWENTY-FOUR

Dot Con- and Dot -ing

Another extremely valuable abbreviating device in Pitmans Shorthand is the use of a light dot—at the beginning of an outline to represent the syllables *con-* or *com-*, and at the end of an outline to represent the word-ending *-ing*. Note the compact forms of the following outlines, made possible by the use of the dot:

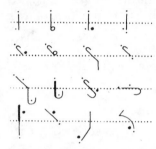

commit, commits, committee, committing

complete, completes, completed, completing

competition, condition, completion, connection

dating, paying, teaching, hearing

Syllable Con-

As illustrated above, the syllables *con-* and *com-* are represented initially by a dot. When occurring medially, either in an outline or a phrase, these syllables (and also *cog-*) are indicated by writing the part of the outline or phrase following the *con-*, etc., close to the preceding part, as in: *reconsider*, *uncommon*, *discomfort*, *uncontrolled*, *recognize*, *recommend;* and *in control*, *in connection*, *we have considered*, *we shall continue.*

Word-ending -ing

Final *-ing* may, as shown above, be represented by a light dot. There are thus two methods of representing

115

-ing, the stroke and the dot. The stroke is more generally used, but the dot is written in the following cases:

(1) After light straight downstrokes and downward **R**, as: ⟍ *paying*, ⟋ *touching*, ⟍ *hearing;*

(2) After circles, loops or hooks where the stroke cannot be conveniently written, as: ⟍ *dancing*, ⟍ *posting*, ⌐ *coughing*, ⟍ *running*, ⌒ *mentioning;*

(3) After half-length and double-length strokes, when no clear angle would result from the use of the stroke, as: ⟍ *meeting*, ⟍ *motoring*, ⟩ *budgeting.* Note ⟍ *ending*, ⌒ *lettering*, and ⟍ *cutting*, where the angle is quite clear.

(4) Generally after Short Forms, as: ⟍ *thinking*, ⟍ *coming*, ⟍ *giving*, ⟍ *informing.* The stroke is, however, preferable in a few cases, as: ⟍ *having*, ⌐ *doing*, ⟍ *being*, ⌒ *calling*, ⟍ *surprising.*

Word-ending -ings

Final *-ings* is represented by a light dash, and it is used in accordance with the same rules as the dot *-ing*: ⟍ *hearings*, ⟋ *winnings*, ⌒ *meetings.*

PRACTICE EIGHTY (Key on p. 158)
Read and copy several times

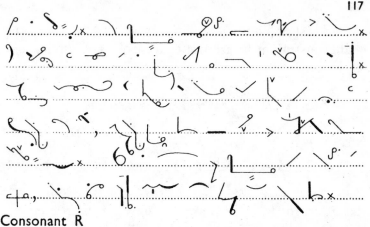

Consonant R

You are already familiar with the use, for vowel indication purposes, of the two forms for R. In order to obtain maximum facility of outline, however, the upward form ╱ *Ray* is sometimes used regardless of the presence or absence of a vowel. Read and copy several times the illustrative outlines given with the following rules:

(1) *Ray* is used at the beginning of an outline when followed by │ │ ╱ ╱ ⌒ ⌐ and ⌐, as in: ╱ *artist*, ╱ *arrayed*, ╱ *arch*, ╱ *urge*, ╱ *earth*, ╱ *article*. A very little experiment will show you that the upward form is preferable in these cases.

(2) *Ray* is used at the end of an outline:

(a) Following a straight upstroke, as: ╱ *where*, ╱ *aware*, ╱ *rear*, ═╱ *carrier*;

(b) Generally after two downstrokes, as: ╲ *prepare*, ╱ *Shakespeare*. The downward R is more facile, however, in such forms as: ╲ *pinafore*, ╲ *persevere*.

(c) After a curve and circle, such as 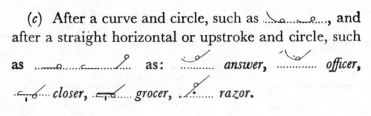, and after a straight horizontal or upstroke and circle, such as .... as: .... *answer*, ... *officer*, ... *closer*, ... *grocer*, ... *razor*.

Final RD

In a few cases final RD is represented by *Ray* halved, as in: .... *coloured*, ... *preferred*, ... *foundered*, where the upward form is more facile and more legible. Generally, however, final RD is represented by Downward R halved and thickened, as in: .... *feared*, ... *tired*, ... *squared*.

Past Tenses

When the Doubling Principle is used in the present tense of a verb, the Halving Principle is used for the past tense, as in: .... *wonder*, ... *wondered*; .... *thunder*, ... *thundered*; .... *tender*, ... *tendered*; .... *matter*, ... *mattered*.

Half-length T or D is disjoined following another T or D, as in: .... *dated*, ... *treated*.

Short Forms

To be copied and memorized:

.... *difficult*, ... *difficulty*, ... *larger*, ... *largely*, ... *especial/ly*, ... *inspect/ed/ion*, ... *responsible/ility*, ... *representative*, ... *financial/ly*.

Phrases

Read and copy:

_____ we were, _____ they were, _____ you were, _____ if you were, _____ for your consideration, _____ I shall consider, _____ if you will continue, _____ in connection with, _____ your requirements, _____ it is required, _____ railway company, _____ new railways, _____ railway ticket.

Note the change of form for the representation of *were* in these phrases, and also the use of the intersected *Ray* to represent the words *require*, *required*, *requirement*, and *railway*.

PRACTICE EIGHTY-ONE (Key on p. 159)

Read and copy several times

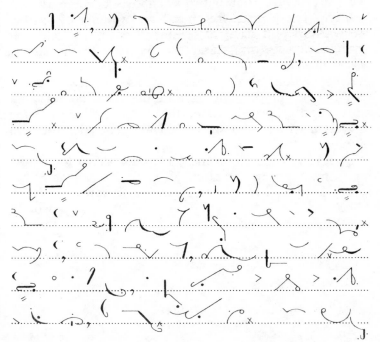

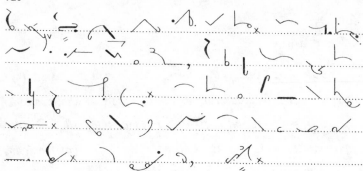

Dictation Test Eleven

First take this Test from slow dictation. Then, after checking your outlines from the Key on p. 159, try to write the test within two minutes.

When we considered the various seasons of the year and[10] contemplated their different moods, we wondered which we preferred, and[20] found it difficult to decide. We were aware that with[30] each season there is new beauty. There is the freshness[40] and wonder of Spring, the warmth and scent of summer[50] days, the coloured loveliness of Autumn, and the purity of[60] the snowy wastes of Winter.

Each season of the year[70] seems to answer some requirement of our minds and of[80] our bodies and, admitting this, we concluded that we loved[90] the passing days as a whole, and we ceased to[100] consider them in division.

To find in each day some[110] common cause for rejoicing, some vital appreciation of Nature, whatever[120] her mood, is to find in life a joyous and[130] rare happiness.

(132 words)

LESSON TWENTY-FIVE

Prefixes and Suffixes

Facile and brief outlines are obtained by using special abbreviations for very common syllables occurring at the beginning or at the end of words. These special "prefixes" and "suffixes" are set out here, and should be thoroughly memorized, as their use will save you much valuable time in practical shorthand writing.

Prefixes

Syllable	Sign	As in outlines
Accom-	.... joined or disjoined	accomplish, accompany
Intro-	(sign)	introduce, introspection
Magna- Magne- Magni-	disjoined	magnetize, magnificent
Trans-	(sign)	transfer, transport *Note:* transit, in which the inclusion of ...... is preferable.
Self-	disjoined	self-made, self-help

Syllable	Sign	As in outlines
Self-con-	....ᴏ.... in the position of *con-* dot	⌇ self-control, ⌡ self-contained
In- (Before Str, Skr and H)	⌡ ᴌ ⟋	⌡ instrument, ⌿ in-scription, ∠ inhabit
		Note: Negative words are written with stroke N: ⟋ *inhospitable.*
Ir-, Il-	(*a*) Downward form:	⌐ irresolute, ⌐ irresistible, illimitable
		Compare: ⌐ resolute, limitable
	(*b*) Repetition of consonant:	⌐ illegal, ⌐ irredeemable
		Compare: ⌐ legal, redeemable
Im-, In-	Repetition of consonant	⌐ immaterial, unnecessary
		Compare: material, necessary
Con-, Com-	As shown in Lesson Twenty-four	

Suffixes

Syllable	Sign	As in outlines
-ality -ility -arity, etc.	Disjoining of preceding stroke	formality, possibility, regularity, majority, novelty
-logical/ly	Disjoined /.	psychological, geological
-ment		agreement, sentiment, announcement, pavement *Note:* The form is used when does not join easily.
-mental/ly -mentality	Disjoined	fundamental, instrumental
-ly	(a) joined or disjoined	safely, mainly, friendly, particularly *Note:* L is disjoined to obtain a more facile or distinctive outline.
	(b) Hook L	deeply, respectfully, respectively

124

Syllable	Sign	As in outlines
-ship	╱ joined **or** disjoined	friendship, ownership, hardship
-fulness	disjoined	hopefulness, carefulness
-lessness -lousness	disjoined	hopelessness, carelessness, credulousnes
-ward -wart		backward, stalwart
-yard		backyard, shipyard
-ing -ings		

As shown in Lesson Twenty-four

PRACTICE EIGHTY-TWO (Key on p. 160)

Read and copy several times

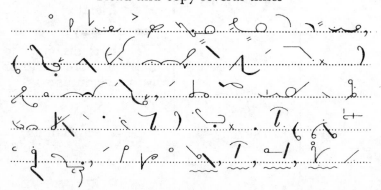

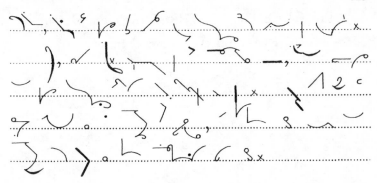

Short Forms

To be copied and memorized:

instructive, _instruction_, _description_, _demonstration_, _expenditure_, _expensive_, _irresponsible_, _introduction_, _intelligent_, _intelligence_, _investigation_, _justification_, _uniform/ity_.

Note: Short Forms are also known as Grammalogues and Contractions, the Grammalogues consisting of those Short Forms composed of one sign or stroke only, and the Contractions those using more than one stroke.

Phrases

Read and copy:

yours sincerely, _very sincerely_, _yours very sincerely_, _I would_, _they would_, _we would_, _I have concluded_, _come to the conclusion_, _I have come to the conclusion_, _new department_, _forwarding department_.

Note the use of _way_ halved for _would_, the use of the principle of omission, and the use of the intersected D for _department_.

PRACTICE EIGHTY-THREE (Key on p. 160)

Read and copy several times

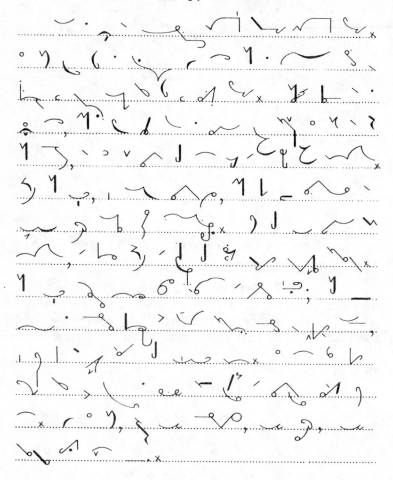

REVISION FIVE

You have now reached the end of the theory of Pitmans Shorthand. In the course of Lessons 21–25 you have learned:

SHUN HOOK as: ___ *action,* ___ *occasions,* ___ *exception,* ___ *suppression,* ___ *affection,* ___ *location,* ___ *irritation,* ___ *emotions,* ___ *illusions,* ___ *mentioning,* ___ *supposition,* ___ *indecision,* ___ *transition.*

UPWARD SH as: ___ *fish,* ___ *vicious,* ___ *dash,* ___ *brush,* ___ *trash,* ___ *sugar,* ___ *shiver.*

SHR, SHL as: ___ *fisher,* ___ *pressure,* ___ *official,* ___ *palatial.*

-UATION as: ___ *situation,* ___ *intuition,* but ___ *accentuation,* ___ *perpetuation.*

SEMICIRCLE W as: ___ *walk,* ___ *women,* ___ *work,* ___ *worth,* ___ *frequently,* ___ *twelve,* ___ *herewith,* ___ *Wordsworth,* ___ *quality,* ___ *qualify.*

EXTENDED USE OF STROKE S as: ___ *science,* ___ *suicide,* ___ *joyous,* ___ *fatuous.*

CIRCLE and STROKE S for -Sess as: ___ *possess,* ___ *process.*

EXTENDED USE OF CONSONANT RAY as: ___ *artist,* ___ *Archie,* ___ *origin,* ___ *where,* ___ *prepare,* ___ *answer,* ___ *preferred,* ___ *coloured.*

USE OF HALVING PRINCIPLE IN PAST TENSES as: ___ *wondered,* ___ *thundered,* ___ *tendered,* ___ *mattered.*

VOWEL INDICATION as: ___ *test,* ___ *testy;* ___ *gas,* ___ *gassy;* ___ *sack,* ___ *ask;* ___ *store,* ___ *story;*

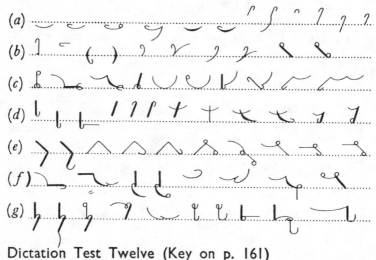

jeer, *cheery;* *rack,* *ark;* *lamb,* *elm;* *long,* *along;* *fun,* *funny;* *pen,* *penny;* *puff,* *puffy;* *men,* *many;* *poster,* *pastry,* *winter,* *wintry.*

PREFIXES AND SUFFIXES—the use of special abbreviations for common syllables occurring at the beginning or at the end of words, as illustrated in Lesson Twenty-four and in this Lesson.

Short Forms

(To be used as a Facility Drill)

(a)

(b)

(c)

(d)

(e)

(f)

(g)

Dictation Test Twelve (Key on p. 161)

Write the following Test from dictation, attempting to take down the 227 words within three minutes.

A lonely fisherman was standing on the river bank. He[10] seemed to me, as he stood there quite alone and[20] accompanied only by his own thoughts and perhaps an odd[30] fish or two, to be representative of all fishing

enthusiasts[40] the world over. To me his pastime seemed
fatuous; but[50] no doubt he himself found in it an escape
from[60] other duties, or perhaps he believed that he was
pursuing[70] an art, a science even, of a particularly high
order.[80] I am mentioning all this because, in the course
of[90] my casual walk that morning, I myself became
caught up[100] in the process of fishing. I long ago came
to[110] the conclusion that I possessed a strong power of
intuition,[120] and my intuition told me then that if I
went[130] near that lonely man I would become involved
in something[140] I very sincerely wished to avoid. I
therefore turned aside[150] and began to climb over the
old stile near the[160] great elm tree. Suddenly, however,
I heard what sounded to[170] my ears remarkably like the
controlled suppression of a frightened[180] cry for assistance.
In a moment of indecision I turned,[190] and with some
surprise saw the man struggling in the[200] water. As I
dashed across the meadow I had time[210] to reflect that
I had not reckoned on fishing a[220] man out of the water
that morning.   (227 words)

KEYS

(Counted in ten's for dictation purposes)

PRACTICE ONE

(a) pay, paid, day, date, bay, bait, age, page, (b) tow, towed (toad),[10] bow, boat, Tay, tape, obey, poach. (16 words)

PRACTICE TWO

(a) pay, pays, Tay, stay, Joe, chose, oats, stow, sage, (b) tape,[10] tapes, paid, spade, spades, boat, boats, space, soap. (18 words)

PRACTICE THREE

(a) Pay it. It is paid. Joe paid it. Pay it[10] to-day. (b) Date it to-day. It is to-day's date. It is[20] to be paid to-day. (c) The boat is his. It is[30] Joe's boat. Joe chose it. (d) It is a spade. The[40] spade is Joe's. It is to be his to-day. (49 words)

PRACTICE FOUR

(a) debt, debts, jet, jets, jut, juts, judge, judges, bet, bets.[10] (b) such, does, said, touch, touches, set, sets, sedate, bus, Tess.[20] (c) The debt is paid. Ted paid it to Joe. Ted[30] set it up. (d) Tess is to stay to-day. Is Tess[40] to touch it up? (44 words)

PRACTICE FIVE

(a) safe, safes, save, saves, show, shows, bathe, bathes, shade, shades.[10] (b) foe, photo, fetch, faith, death, fudge, shed, shape, thud, vote.[20] (c) The photo is Joe's. Tess showed it to Ted. It[30] is a photo of his face. (d) The bay is safe.[40] It is safe to bathe to-day. (46 words)

PRACTICE SIX

(a) The photo of Ted is for you. Joe thanks you[10] for it. Is that a photo of you? (b) Have you[20] a set of the photos

130

for the judge? The judge[30] said that you have a set.
(c) That is a safe[40] shade to have. Does that shade fade?
It does fade.[50]   (d) They showed it to you to-day. Joe thinks
that the[60] judge is to publish it for you.   (67 words)

PRACTICE SEVEN

PRACTICE EIGHT

(a) Change the cheque to-day. Thank you for changing
the cheques[10] for the judge. They have enough cheques.
(b) The name of[20] the month is May. The name of the day is[30]
Monday. (c) Have you a set of the photos to show[40] to May?
That set is the same as his. (d) Does[50] May take that set to
the show? You may check[60] the sums for Ted.   (64 words)

PRACTICE NINE

(a) Have you something that may be published in the
Echo[10] to-day? May I take it that much of that page[20] is to be
published on Monday? May I publish any[30] of it on the
date you name? (b) I have to[40] take May to the show on
Monday. It is the[50] custom to take some cheques. (c) Have
you enough cheques in[60] the case? I have nothing in the case
to-day. (d) They[70] came in to-day but I think it may have
no[80] effect on the case.   (84 words)

PRACTICE TEN

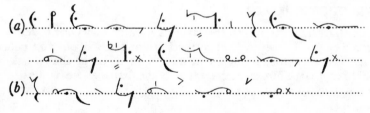

(c)

(d)

Dictation Test Two

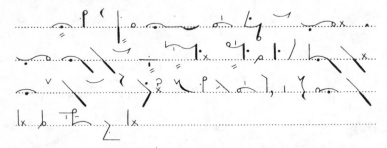

PRACTICE ELEVEN

(a) You may take the case to the judge to-day. The[10] judge has paid for it. (b) Is that case the same[20] as the case that May is taking? (c) It is his[30] custom to make some changes on Monday. Joe has the[40] cheques. (d) I have paid it. I know that I have[50] enough. May I change much of it?

(57 words)

PRACTICE TWELVE

(a) I paid the tax at the bank on Monday. You[10] may add up the sums for Tom. (b) Jack Thomson showed[20] his pass at the docks. Have you bought any of[30] the sets? (c) Tom Jackson is off to the shops. Have[40] you any cheques to change at the bank? (d) The change[50] in the tax may cause Joe to stay at the[60] bank to-day.

(62 words)

PRACTICE THIRTEEN

I shall take the car to the farm as usual,[10] as I wish to fetch some eggs. I wish to[20] get to the farm at four. Tom and you may[30] both come, though you may have to be at the[40] back. I think that Tom is to get off at[50] the bank as he wishes to exchange some forms.

(59 words)

PRACTICE FOURTEEN

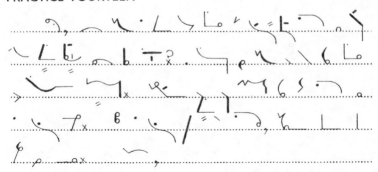

PRACTICE FIFTEEN

(*a*) You may take the car to the farm to-day. Jack[10] can fetch some eggs for you. (*b*) I think that the[20] car has four doors, but I shall check up for[30] you. (*c*) Is it far to the farm? No, you can[40] get to the farm at four. (*d*) Have you got the[50] sets? Does May wish to take them back and exchange[60] them?
(61 words)

PRACTICE SIXTEEN

(*a*) You may take a seat in the office if you[10] wish, and make a copy of the form. (*b*) I think[20] that Eddie may choose to take up the same business[30] as you and Betty. (*c*) It is muddy in the meadow[40] to-day. I shall come up to the City each day.[50] (*d*) I think that Jack is making these sets for Messrs.[60] Dee and Barr. (63 words)

PRACTICE SEVENTEEN

(*a*) They say that they may ask us to teach King[10] to keep the books and check the sums. (*b*) If the[20] baby moves in a minute or so she shall have[30] some food. (*c*) Since it is easy to see that he[40] is poor, I fear that he has no pennies for[50] books. (51 words)

PRACTICE EIGHTEEN

Sirs, Thank you for the four forms that King has[10] given to me to-day. The fact is that I wish[20] to have six copies of the same form, so may[30] I ask if you can get King to make these[40] copies for me? If it is easy for him to[50] make the copies, can King pass them to me in[60] a day or so? I am, (66 words)

PRACTICE NINETEEN

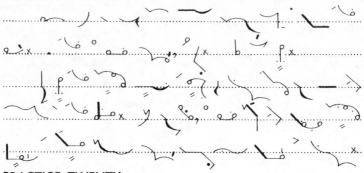

PRACTICE TWENTY

Thank you for the message in which you ask me[10] if the firm has published anything on Exchange since May.[20] The firm has, I fear, published nothing for some months,[30] but it is expected to publish something soon. I have[40] the copy for four books in the office, and I[50] think I can get them in the shops in a[60] month or so. The checking of the pages keeps me[70] busy, and if you think you can aid me I[80] can pass a batch of copy to you for checking.[90]   (90 words)

PRACTICE TWENTY-ONE

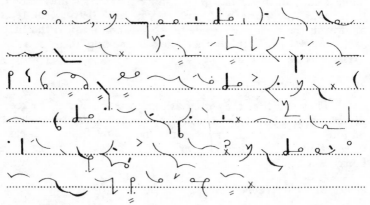

PRACTICE TWENTY-TWO

(a) Yes, I shall be happy to leave a load of[10] coal for you early on Wednesday. (b) I shall look in[20] the windows of the shops to see if I can[30] match that colour. (c) They say that they hope to sell[40] the milk and a heavy load of the meal to-day.[50]   (d) The head of the business is away and I have[60] no details of the sales of these small watches.   (69 words)

PRACTICE TWENTY-THREE

Sir, I spoke to the buyer for Messrs. Miles and[10] Joyce on Wednesday. It seems that it is some time[20] since the firm has sold any of the silk you[30] desire to buy.

They can sell you some lace in[40] the design you name if six inches is wide enough.[50]   As the lace is scarce they hope to know soon[60] if you desire to buy any. They add that they[70] can dye the lace to any shade you like.

I[80] am,   (81 words)

PRACTICE TWENTY-FOUR

I hope you will speak to Doyle on Wednesday as[10] the July sales of silk appear to be much below[20] the usual sales for this season.   I think you should[30] specially ask him to show you the details of all[40] the sales to customers and to show you, too, the[50] details of all that he has bought off the manufacturers[60] since January. We should have all these facts so that[70] we can judge the sales fairly.   (76 words)

PRACTICE TWENTY-FIVE

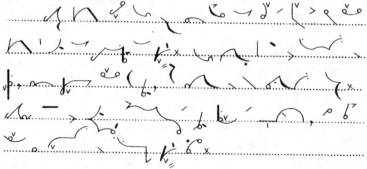

Dictation Test Four

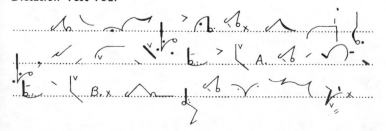

PRACTICE TWENTY-SIX

We rang up on Wednesday to say that we shall[10] be happy to receive the load of rugs to-morrow or[20] on Saturday. If the rugs come by road, we hope[30] that you will see that the lorry leaves the factory[40] in time to reach us early in the day. We[50] hope also that you will ensure that each rug bears[60] the right markings as to size, design, colour, etc.   (69 words)

PRACTICE TWENTY-SEVEN

(*a*) Ask Harry to pass the sack of coal to Lucy[10] or Bess to-morrow. (*b*) That car can carry all of them[20] and we have authority to use it for the purpose.[30] (*c*) Thomas Moore said that he hopes to marry Bessie Oscar[40] early in March.

(43 words)

PRACTICE TWENTY-EIGHT

We thank you for ringing up and we shall be[10] happy to allow you to view the house in Essex[20] Road on Tuesday. The name of the house is South[30] View and from the windows you can see for many[40] miles. Some changes are being carried out but the house[50] should be ready early in the year. We are sorry[60] that we have no smaller house on our books likely[70] to suit you.   (73 words)

PRACTICE TWENTY-NINE

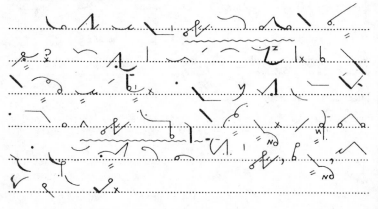

Dictation Test Five

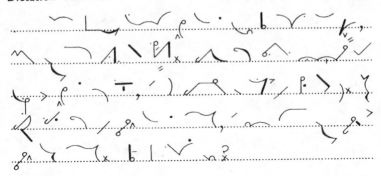

PRACTICE THIRTY

As the swelling on his arm, caused by the mosquito[10] bites, was much less severe, Sydney took a swim in[20] the small lake. The surface was smooth, although the sweep[30] of his arms was soon causing tiny swirls of foam[40] to lap the banks. The sun was low in the[50] sky, and the sweet smell of the July roses was[60] in the air. The coolness was such a relief that[70] Sydney sang aloud from sheer happiness.   (76 words)

PRACTICE THIRTY-ONE

Sweeney insists that the scheme was a decisive success, and[10] says that it shows that it was right for him[20] to resist any changes in policy. Sweeney emphasizes that such[30] successes come seldom in life, and adds that it is[40] now necessary to get the scheme going in all our[50] offices.   (51 words)

PRACTICE THIRTY-TWO

You ask why we have had to refuse the cases[10] of sweets. As we think you know, we bought these[20] cases from you as long ago as February. It is[30] now July and the sweets in the cases are of[40] a very different type from those you showed us at[50] the time. We hope you will dispatch new cases of[60] sweets as soon as possible as we wish to satisfy[70] our customers as well as we can.   (77 words)

138

PRACTICE THIRTY-THREE

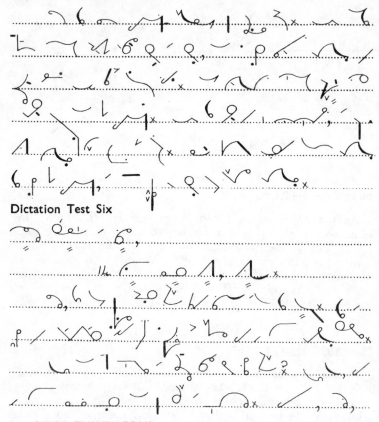

Dictation Test Six

PRACTICE THIRTY-FOUR

Stella passed the day in the new State Gallery, and[10] she states that she is amazed at the beauty and[20] power of Stone's latest masterpieces. His choice of colours in[30] still-life, she says, gives him an effect that is[40] very different from the rest of the show. In Stella's[50] view, Stone is the best living master of this form,[60] and she suggests that he must soon reach the top[70] ranks. (71 words)

PRACTICE THIRTY-FIVE

(a) We are asking Jessie and Bessie to visit us and[10] we hope that Tess comes as well. (b) The dust on[20] the road may make the shiny new car dusty but[30] we can polish it. (*c*) I noticed that some of the[40] steel is going rusty and I think that we should[50] ask the manufacturer why this is so. (57 words)

PRACTICE THIRTY-SIX

Messrs. Masters & Guest,
14 West Road, Stepney.

Sirs, I[10] am happy to inform you that for the first time[20] since February I have now a big stock of steel[30] chests in different sizes. These chests are specially manufactured for[40] such uses as you state, and there is no fear[50] that they will go rusty if exposed to the air[60] for a time. I attach a list of sizes and[70] costs, and I suggest that you inform me as soon[80] as possible as to your desires. I can dispatch any[90] of the chests to you as soon as you wish,[100] this firm to bear all road and insurance costs. All[110] the chests carry our guarantee.

I am, Yours, (118 words)

PRACTICE THIRTY-SEVEN

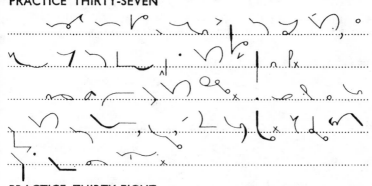

PRACTICE THIRTY-EIGHT

The reason I spoke as I did is that I[10] thought that we should not act now but should wait[20] a little time. It is most necessary that we should[30] read the expert's report. From the facts given in his[40] written report we shall get to know if the results[50] of the tests are good or bad, and we can[60] act on this knowledge. I know that he is operating[70] a system very similar to ours, and it is possible[80] that certain of his methods might be used by us.[90] I have not met him yet, and if you write[100] to him I suggest that you ask him to meet[110] us for lunch. Any day except Wednesday is all right[120] for me. (122 words)

PRACTICE THIRTY-NINE

It is not always easy to get results right away,[10] and that is why I wanted you to send out[20] the first thousand cards in good time. These notices should[30] be followed up very soon indeed if the support aimed[40] at is not received at first. If we failed to[50] make a good start we might lose much support, and[60] I hope you will make certain that all the facts[70] needed are filled in on the cards that you send[80] out. (81 words)

PRACTICE FORTY

If it is wet I sometimes stay in bed and[10] read for hours. I did this last Saturday with the[20] desired result that I quite caught up on the reading[30] of books that I had wanted to read for some[40] time past. I know this sounds lazy but indeed it[50] is not as, apart from reading, I can sort out[60] my thoughts when I am at peace in bed in[70] a way that is not easy when engaged in the[80] mad rush of city life. I admit that there is[90] a limit to the hours that can be passed in[100] this way. There is no doubt, too, about the fact[110] that reading in bed is an art of which not[120] all are masters but I have built up a technique[130] in this field that has satisfied me for years. (139 words)

PRACTICE FORTY-ONE

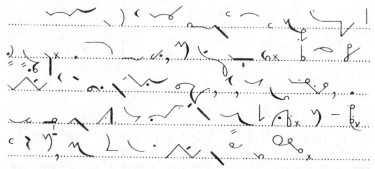

PRACTICE FORTY-TWO

Lucy and Joyce wanted to go out but the night[10] was misty and Dad, who is fussy about them, asked[20] them to stay in the house. So we built up[30] the fire, and had a happy time as Daddy chatted[40] about his fat pigs, almost ready for the market, and[50] swanked about his old sheep, of how their coats must[60] soon be cut, of their weight, and of many similar[70] things. We knew it all, it was the same story[80] that he had related a thousand times, but we enjoyed[90] it just the same.

(94 words)

PRACTICE FORTY-THREE

I have just received a letter from father asking me[10] if I will motor into Manchester after lunch and go[20] with him to the pictures. A very special Nature picture[30] is on show at the Palace, and father thinks that[40] it would be quite nice for me to see it[50] with him and mother. Neither of them usually visits the[60] pictures, and on another day I could do as he[70] suggests but to-day I have too many mail orders to[80] deal with.

(82 words)

PRACTICE FORTY-FOUR

My dear Sir, Thank you for your letter of 14th[10] November. I think there is a lot in what you[20] say in respect of the under-taking named in your letter,[30] and I think we ought to move cautiously in this[40] matter. Would you be so good as to look in[50] at this office soon so that we can discuss the[60] matter fully? I know there is much to be said[70] on both sides, and I have no wish to act[80] hastily or unwisely. Still, I think there is no time[90] to lose as I am being asked by this same[100] firm to put my signature to some forms this month,[110] and as matters are now I have no wish to[120] do so. If you will ring me up and let[130] me know when you can come in, I will be[140] on hand to meet you. Yours,

(146 words)

PRACTICE FORTY-FIVE

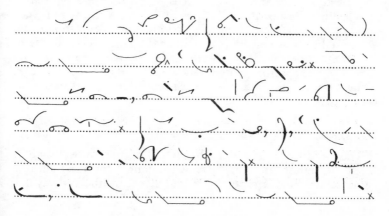

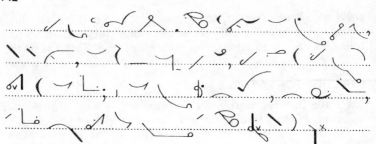

Dictation Test Seven

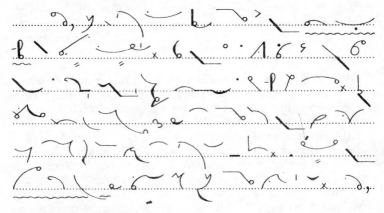

PRACTICE FORTY-SIX

If you wish to make rapid headway in speed writing,[10] as I suppose most of you do, you must accustom[20] yourself to writing lightly and neatly. It is the facile[30] and light style that leads to fast writing. If possible,[40] use a nib that is soft, but not too soft,[50] and that will yield a little. You should use a[60] pencil only if you have no nib that writes nicely[70] enough for your purposes. If you write as lightly as[80] you ought, no marks of your writing should show on[90] the back of the page. Your hand should skim the[100] surface of the page as lightly as a fairy.   (109 words)

PRACTICE FORTY-SEVEN

They said that there was a heavy fall of the[10] railway banks. I left the house and moved slowly along[20] the road until I came to the Red House that[30] had stood by the railway for so long. I knocked[40] at the door but as I could make out no[50] sound, no sign of life inside, I made my way[60] cautiously to the back. It was moonlight, and I could[70] see the railway banks slip and slide as they still[80] fell away. Most of the cabbage patch that had delighted[90] old Tom was falling in, and I feared for the[100] safety of the house. Undecided what to do next, I[110] stood there for a minute or two, but suddenly the[120] very path started to part under my feet, and an[130] awful slit appeared. I rushed back to the road, and[140] into the fields, away, away from the awful sight. Yet[150] I had to watch. Slowly, slowly the Red House swayed,[160] uncannily, terrifyingly, until with a mighty sound it fell and[170] disappeared from my sight. (174 words)

PRACTICE FORTY-EIGHT

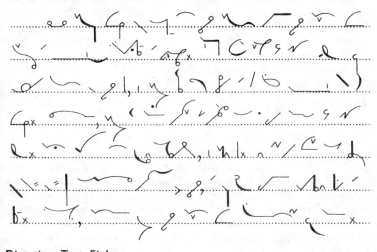

Dictation Test Eight

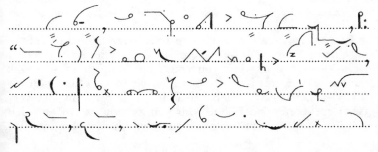

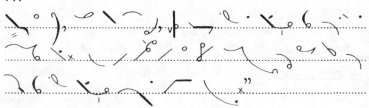

PRACTICE FORTY-NINE

My dear Matthew, Thank you for your letter. Knowing your[10] views, I think it will be a real relief to[20] you when I say that I am following your suggestion,[30] and sending out our magazines much earlier this month. Unfortunately,[40] there is a really serious lack of good material, and[50] I should like to know if you have any ideas[60] as to how we can secure useful copy. Lewis was[70] saying recently that our rates are the lowest for any[80] magazine of this sort, and I think we shall have[90] to give serious thought to the matter of revising our[100] scale. I hope that I shall be seeing you soon.[110]

Meantime, I wish you good luck. Yours, (117 words)

PRACTICE FIFTY

You will be happy to know that I am moving[10] from my house in Holmes Road. I have bought a[20] house on the lower slopes of Hobhouse Hill, following father's[30] suggestion. I really wanted a house a little higher up[40] the hill, but father said he thought *High Hills*—the[50] name of my new house—was very good value for[60] the money. Cynthia and Owen are both happy when hiking,[70] and I expect that on many a sunny day we[80] shall be up on the hills, thoroughly enjoying life. If[90] you can face the uphill road, I hope you will[100] come to see me soon. (105 words)

PRACTICE FIFTY-ONE

I was very much interested to have your letter as[10] I have not heard from you for several months. Several[20] times I have asked myself what you could be doing[30] and why you sent no letters. It is really good[40] news to hear that you are taking a house on[50] Hobhouse Hill. It is certainly not very far from here,[60] and I shall visit you as soon as I hear[70] that you are fixed up. Hobhouse is an ideal village[80] because it is still unspoilt. I hope you will send[90] me word when you are ready for me to pay[100] you a visit. By the way, Lewis also lives at[110] Hobhouse, quite by himself, and you may wish to get[120] in touch with him.   (124 words)

PRACTICE FIFTY-TWO

PRACTICE FIFTY-THREE

My dear Bruce, I have brought your offer of April[10] first to the notice of my Board, and they agree[20] to the terms you suggest for the sale of your[30] products to this firm.

The respect in which they differ[40] from you is on the matter of the price at[50] which the goods should be sold to the public. They[60] have therefore asked me to inform you that, in their[70] view, the present high prices ruling for labour and materials[80] necessitate an increased selling price. I think this is a[90] true analysis, and I trust you will agree. Can you[100] come in on either Friday or Saturday next, bringing all[110] the necessary papers and figures with you, so that we[120] can try to reach a mutually satisfactory figure? Yours,   (129 words)

PRACTICE FIFTY-FOUR

Dear Margaret, As a writer of this system it is[10] in your immediate interests now to take great care to[20] write carefully and properly. If you are careless now it[30] will be far from easy for you to write really[40] satisfactory notes later on when you try to write at[50] higher speeds. I trust therefore that you will be true[60] to your best interests and produce notes that are a[70] credit to yourself and to the system.

You should do[80] some theory and some speed every day, either writing an[90] exercise from this book or doing a facility drill—or,[100] better still, doing both. During the writing of the exercise[110] or drill, you should try to write a note that[120] does not differ very much from the style used in[130] these pages, either as to size or thickness.

With best[140] wishes and love, Chris. (144 words)

PRACTICE FIFTY-FIVE

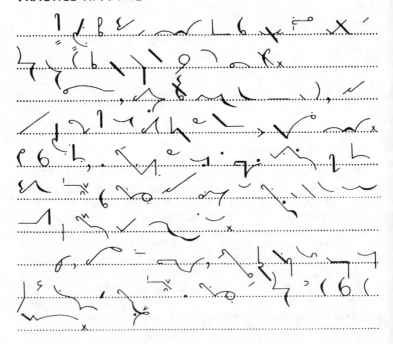

PRACTICE FIFTY-SIX

You will realize the full value of this new time-[10]saving device when you picture such forms as *straight* and[20] *spring*. If we leave out the vowel sign and write[30] only *str–t*, we have satisfactorily indicated four longhand letters in[40] that little sign; yet it is neat and rapidly formed.[50] The form *spr–ng*, without the vowel sign, has in it[60] five longhand letters, but it can be formed with a[70] light and rapid sweep. If we think it necessary to[80] show the vowel sign in either or both of these[90] cases, the dot can be added with no loss of[100] time.

You should make full use of all the time-[110]saving devices taught in these Lessons. There is a real[120] reason for each of them, and the better your knowledge[130] of them the higher is your speed likely to be.[140]   (140 words)

PRACTICE FIFTY-SEVEN

After strolling along the High Street, I kept straight on[10] and soon reached the little stream. It was a lovely[20] Spring day, almost as hot as in the early summer[30] months, and the water was bright and smooth. It was[40] a day for happiness. The birds expressed their joy by[50] singing loudly as the branches of the trees swayed lightly[60] in the breeze. I expressed my joy by allowing my[70] anger to die away. No longer could I bear a[80] grudge, unjust as everything seemed. Sooner would I suffer myself,[90] I said to the unlistening water.   (96 words)

PRACTICE FIFTY-EIGHT

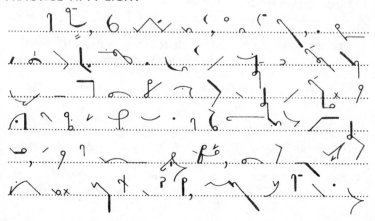

PRACTICE FIFTY-NINE

We hope that you have now reached the stage when[10] you can write notes neatly and at a rate of[20] at least fifty or sixty words a minute. If you[30] have followed out the suggestions made in each Lesson for[40] Facility Drills and if you have had the services of[50] another person to dictate the exercises to you, you will[60] no doubt have made quite rapid progress. Most of you[70] who are studying from this book wish to write as[80] well as to read the system being taught, and it[90] is not likely that you will argue with us when[100] we stress the fact that the easiest way to get[110] up to a higher speed of writing is to do[120] lots of writing, to copy out all of the exercises,[130] to take notes regularly, and to do the facility drills.[140]   (140 words)

PRACTICE SIXTY

From the examples given you will see that the L[10] Hook is similar to the R Hook in that it[20] may be used when the sound of L comes immediately[30] after another letter, as in PL, KL, or FL, or[40] it may be used for a syllable, such as -BLE,[50] -NAL, or -FUL. On the other hand, the L Hook[60] is different from the R Hook in the particular respect[70] that the Hook for L is written on the same[80] side of straight strokes as the Circle S, and the[90] Hook for R is written on the opposite side of[100] straight strokes from the Circle S.

The following pairs illustrate[110] this difference: *praise, place; crows, close; impress, implies; paper, table.*[120]

In the case of other strokes, the R Hook is[130] small and the L Hook is fatter, and this difference[140] must always be clearly indicated. Note the difference in the[150] size of the hooks in the following cases: *offer, fly;*[160] *finer, final; driver, beautiful.*

                    (164 words)

PRACTICE SIXTY-ONE

It may be of interest for you to study the[10] following sets of characters, because it is pleasant not only[20] to know a rule, but to realize *why* there is[30] such a rule: *sup, supper, supple; set, setter, settle; sick,*[40] *sicker, sickle.* These examples illustrate as clearly as any words[50] could do why it is necessary to show both circle[60] and hook in the case of the L Hook, and[70] only the circle in the case of the R Hook.[80]

Because the circle is written on the side of the[90] stroke opposite to the normal Circle S, it is clear[100] to the reader that the sound of R is included;[110] but in the case of the L Hook, which is[120] written on the same side of the stroke as the[130] Circle S, it is not possible for the reader to[140] know that the sound of L is included unless both[150] circle and hook are clearly represented, as in *supply* and[160] *settle*. (161 words)

PRACTICE SIXTY-TWO

PRACTICE SIXTY-THREE

On Thursday the weather was so hot and fresh that[10] my brother and I decided to keep Friday free from[20] study and to go for a picnic by the river;[30] but the weather is nothing if not freakish. When the[40] alarm roused us at six, we threw off the sheets[50] and leapt out of bed only to discover that it[60] was a dull and wet day.

"What a dreadful day!"[70] grumbled Fred. "A day for a novel by the fire,[80] not for a picnic by the river." And so saying,[90] he snuggled back under the bed-covers, and before I[100] could reply he was fast asleep. (106 words)

PRACTICE SIXTY-FOUR

With many people travel books rival novels in their power[10] of holding attention and interest. To hear of another person[20] travelling across Africa, flying to Australia, or sailing the South[30] Seas, can kindle a flame in their hearts. It is[40] not possible for everybody to travel to far places, but[50] the flame can be kept glowing by reading of the[60] journeys made by other travellers. Through books people who may[70] never hold a rifle can share in big game shooting;[80] people who in their whole lives may never travel on[90] a big liner can follow the flight of the latest[100] model flying boat as it crosses thousands of miles of[110] sea. Those who never rode on horseback can travel by[120] pack-mule through desert and valley. (126 words)

PRACTICE SIXTY-FIVE

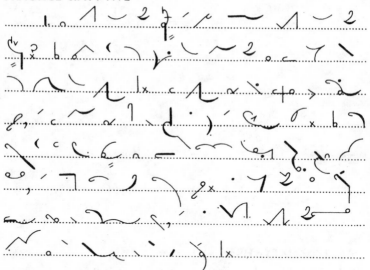

PRACTICE SIXTY-SIX

Perhaps I ought to begin at the beginning and tell[10] you how it happened that I was on the train[20] that evening. As you know, I have a cottage in[30] the country, as well as a house in town. I[40] had attended to several outstanding matters in the early afternoon;[50] then, finding myself free, although it was only three o'clock,[60] I decided to run down into the country and have[70] a look round my place. I have rather a lot[80] of land, and I knew that the ground behind the[90] house ought to be given more attention. I usually depend[100] upon the services of a couple of men in this[110] respect.　　　(111 words)

PRACTICE SIXTY-SEVEN

The General Iron & Steel Company, 14 Trent Street, Glasgow.[10]

Gentlemen, We have to inform you that your Mr. Lines[20] called here yesterday, as arranged, and showed us your most[30] modern pattern of washing machine. Although the situation in which[40] we find ourselves at the moment does not allow of[50] the immediate purchase of one or more of your machines,[60] we shall keep the matter in mind. Incidentally, the price[70] is several pounds higher than we had been led to[80] expect, but we understand that a satisfactory allowance can be[90] made upon old machines, if returned to you. Yours faithfully,[100]

(100 words)

PRACTICE SIXTY-EIGHT

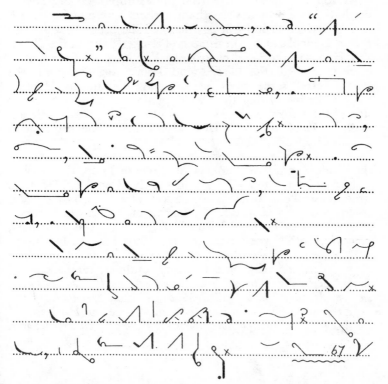

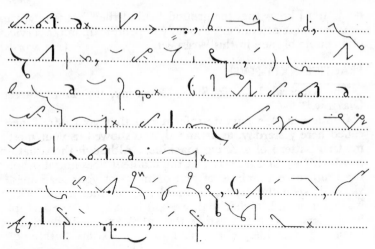

PRACTICE SIXTY-NINE

As you will have noted from the examples given above,[10] the F/V Hook provides shorthand writers with another time-[20] saving device. You have now learned the proper use of[30] the R and L Hooks at the beginning of strokes[40] and of the N and F/V Hooks at the[50] end of strokes. You have also learned the correct use[60] of the Circles and Loops, together with the Hooks. In[70] some cases, as you have found, the Hook is indicated[80] by writing the Circle, or the Loop, on the same[90] side of the stroke as the Hook; in other cases,[100] the Circle S and the Hook are both clearly shown.[110] The principle is quite easily learnt, however.

When a Circle[120] or Loop is added to a straight stroke on the[130] side opposite to the normal Circle or Loop, the Hook[140] can safely be omitted. This applies to the R and[150] N Hooks to straight strokes, so that you may write:[160] *stray, sweater, stouter, dance, danced, dances.* In the case of[170] all hooks to curves and in the case of the[180] L and F/V Hooks to straight strokes, however, both[190] the Circle and the Hook have to be shown, as[200] otherwise the outline would suggest only a plain Circle S.[210] Practise writing the following outlines, taking care to show the[220] differences: *set, settle, safe, safer, soon, sooner, sieve, civil, mice,[230] mines, mills, millions, dice, dives, cause, coughs.*

In the middle[240] of outlines, too, both Circle and Hook should be shown,[250] as in: *possible, industry, explain, decipher, designer.*

(257 words)

PRACTICE SEVENTY

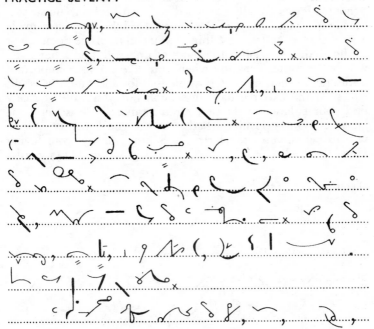

PRACTICE SEVENTY-ONE

My dear McGuire, I am very interested in the question[10] of the issue of your new quarterly periodical, *Queries and*[20] *Questions*, and I shall eagerly await the first issue in[30] December next. While I think that your idea is a[40] good one, however, I feel that you should perhaps have[50] a fuller and clearer understanding of all that is required[60] to make such a periodical a success. I am willing[70] to do all I can to help you, as requested,[80] and it would be well, in my opinion, for us[90] to discuss various points. I suggest that we meet together[100] for lunch one day, and I would like to bring[110] Mr. White along with me, as he knows a great[120] deal about such questions. Can you ring me up one[130] afternoon, and let me know when you are free to[140] lunch with us? Very truly yours, (146 words)

PRACTICE SEVENTY-TWO

Dear Queenie, I was very pleased to have your letter[10] yesterday, but I must admit that I was very surprised[20] to learn that you are no longer at the English[30] Language Training School. I was equally surprised to learn the[40] circumstances that led to your leaving. However, I think you[50] have made a wise choice, as I do not think[60] you can improve upon a post as shorthand writer in[70] the Bank of England, and I hope you will be[80] extremely happy when you take up your important duties next[90] month. It is possible that for a few months you[100] will miss the carefree days of school, but you will[110] quickly find your balance in the new circumstances. Please let[120] me know as soon as possible whether or not you[130] will be able to visit us before you leave for[140] the South. Always your loving Uncle Wilfred. (147 words)

Dictation Test Ten

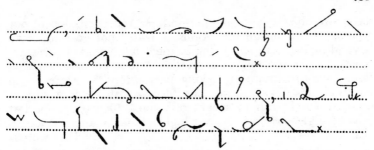

PRACTICE SEVENTY-THREE

From the outlines which have been used in this Lesson,[10] you will observe that the Shun Hook has a tendency[20] to shun strokes and vowel signs. It seems not to[30] like its fellows. For instance, the Shun Hook turns away[40] from the last vowel sign when added to a plain[50] straight stroke, and in this way it helps the shorthand[60] writer to know on which side of the stroke the[70] vowel occurs, even though the sign is not shown in[80] the outline. The following pairs of outlines illustrate this: *education*,[90] *diction; occasion, action; operation, portion.*

The Shun Hook also shuns[100] other hooks, as well as the circles and loops, because[110] it turns away from any attachment at the beginning of[120] the stroke to which it is added. Again the following[130] pairs of outlines illustrate this: *exception, expression, station, suppression; seclusion,*[140] *secretion.*

In spite, however, of this faculty for avoiding its[150] fellow-signs, the Shun Hook has something about it that[160] makes shorthand writers regard it with affection as a valuable[170] possession, a very useful addition to their shorthand knowledge.

(179 words)

PRACTICE SEVENTY-FOUR

I think we may all find some cause for satisfaction[10] in the present situation of our organization. While I do[20] not this morning wish to suggest that we have, through[30] our actions during the past year, reached a state of[40] perfection in our operations, I certainly do feel that our[50] methods of distribution, and of shop operation generally, show such[60] a marked improvement over those previously used that I can[70] with truth say that we are one step nearer to[80] perfection. I do not expect that any of you here[90] this morning will take exception to this modest summary of[100] the position or will

have any objection to this particular[110] representation of our affairs. As to future operations, I will[120] not go into detail beyond saying that, according to the[130] latest trade figures, we have every reason to give expression[140] to a feeling of satisfaction. We are, however, taking precautions[150] to strengthen our position in every way possible, and this[160] is a subject upon which I wish to speak to[170] you. Our profit for last year at £52,000[180] was £4000 higher than for the previous[190] year.
(191 words)

PRACTICE SEVENTY-FIVE

It gives me much satisfaction this morning to be able[10] to say, and to say with truth, that all divisions[20] of our organization are in full and satisfactory operation. A[30] further cause for satisfaction is that relations between the men[40] and the management have never been better than they are[50] at present. Indeed, careful observation of all the facts leads[60] us to the belief that the nation is now in[70] a more favourable position than has been the case for[80] many years. We venture, therefore, to hope that we may[90] be able to look for some reduction next Spring in[100] the high rate of taxation now ruling. High taxation of[110] the kind now in operation cripples effort and acts as[120] an undesirable restriction on extension and expansion of activities generally.[130]
(130 words)

PRACTICE SEVENTY-SIX

Dear Mr. Fisher, Thank you for your letter of yesterday[10] and for the valuable information with regard to the present[20] position of the Education Authority. In my opinion several of[30] these matters affect the nation as a whole and ought[40] to have attention on a national basis. For instance, when[50] a proficient body such as ours has not sufficient staff[60] to carry on in a thoroughly efficient manner, I certainly[70] think the deficiency should be made public. The education of[80] our children should be regarded as a national investment and,[90] having regard to the vital importance of the matter, I[100] propose to approach several influential friends and ask them to[110] take appropriate action.

In regard to your suggestion for a[120] fishing expedition, I think the advantages of your proposals are[130] such that they will meet with unanimous acceptance from all[140] to whom an invitation is sent. There can be no[150] doubt that you will obtain the co-operation of the owners[160] of the fishing rights in the district if they are[170] at all sensible. With kind regards, I am, Yours truly,[180]   (180 words)

PRACTICE SEVENTY-SEVEN

Dear Sir or Madam, There are times when a man[10] or a woman needs a doctor, even if it is[20] only to be toned up. Men and women sometimes become[30] run down or weak, and at such times a little[40] care and attention can work wonders. In the same way,[50] your wireless set sometimes requires the services of a radio[60] doctor if it is to do its best work. It[70] frequently happens that when one enters a home one is[80] aware of the poor quality of the reception over the[90] wireless set. Reception seems weak or distorted, and one has[100] the impression that the set is worn out and worth[110] very little. Actually, however, it is not infrequently the case[120] that the wireless set itself is of good quality and[130] is worthy of skilled treatment. A qualified dealer could, in[140] less than a week, overhaul the set and return it[150] worth apparently twice as much. Every set should be given[160] attention at least once in twelve months. Why not let[170] us test your wireless set and tell you whether or[180] not the quality of your reception can be improved? Just[190] ring up Cromwell 777 and we will do[200] the rest. Yours faithfully,   (204 words)

PRACTICE SEVENTY-EIGHT

It is possible that you may have asked yourself occasionally[10] why you have been asked to memorize the Short Forms[20] given with each Lesson while you have been told only[30] to read and to copy the phrases. The reason is[40] really quite simple. The Short Forms are specially abbreviated outlines[50] for the most frequently used words in the English language.[60] They will occur very frequently in the course of any[70] notetaking you may do, and it is therefore in your[80] best interests to have a perfect knowledge of them. They[90] must be learned by heart so that they can be[100] used without hesitation and written within the least time possible.[110] The phrases, on the other hand, are more variable, and[120] there is not the same hard and fast usage. Let[130] us take one example, the four words: *It is most*[140] *important*. You may hear these words in the course of[150] dictation, and write: *It-is most-important*. Someone else may[160] hear them, and write: *It-is-most important*. The response[170] of a third person may be to write: *It-is-*[180]*most-important.* All three attempts are acceptable; nevertheless, the third[190] person has, of course, achieved the best possible phrase. Then,[200] too, a phrase may be broken up by an interpolated[210] word, as: *It is certainly most important.* The shorthand writer[220] must be ready to adjust the phrase to his immediate[230] needs.

Notwithstanding these remarks, however, you should certainly endeavour to[240] use all the phrases which have been taught within the[250] covers of this book. Still more important is it that[260] you should know the *principles* underlying the phrases, so that[270] you can apply the principles to other phrases.

(278 words)

PRACTICE SEVENTY-NINE

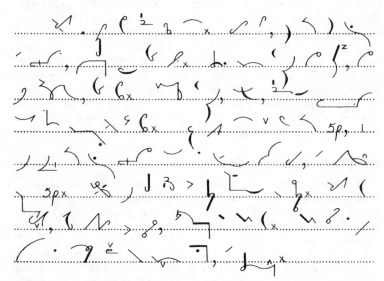

PRACTICE EIGHTY

A company such as ours, in common with other concerns[10] of a similar nature, has heavy commitments, and it is[20] always a source of comfort and satisfaction to contemplate a[30] sound balance-sheet at the conclusion of the year. We[40] are happy to-day to be considering such a balance-sheet.[50] Your Directors exercise constant care in the control of the[60] company. They are always concerned with costs, and a continuous[70] watch is kept on prices of all commodities. In this[80] connection,

I must mention that at present all companies of[90] our type are meeting with severe competition from abroad, and[100] if this competition continues it may give rise to the[110] undesirable practice of price-cutting. This is a matter to[120] which the Directors are paying constant and close attention, comparing[130] sales of different commodities and noting important changes in public[140] demand. (141 words)

PRACTICE EIGHTY-ONE

Dear Archie, I was very interested in your letter which[10] reached me on the morning of my birthday. While thanking[20] you for your good wishes, I must add that I[30] congratulate you on your recent successes. You say that you[40] have not yet been to the Constable Galleries. I really[50] must urge you to go and inspect the work of[60] Arthur Congreve. I am confident that we have in him[70] a new artist of great worth. I was lured into[80] the Galleries rather against my will, but I was so[90] fascinated with Congreve's work that I would not consider leaving[100] until I had completed an inspection of all the rooms.[110] I am sure that, with your expert knowledge, you will[120] have no difficulty in recognizing that Congreve has a larger[130] vision, a deeper awareness of the responsibility of the artist[140] to convey emotion, than can be found anywhere else. I[150] am sufficiently confident of this to prophesy that Congreve will[160] become the representative artist of our times. I am indeed[170] contemplating writing an article about his work, although it is[180] difficult for me to find the time to devote to[190] this interesting theme. My time is largely given up at[200] present to music. Please be sure to ring me up[210] when next you are coming this way. Your sincere friend,[220] Wentworth. (221 words)

Dictation Test Eleven

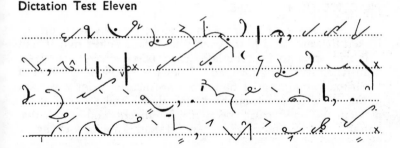

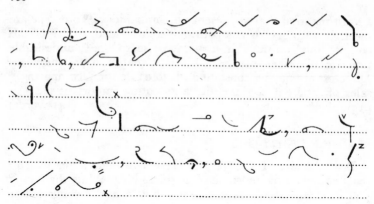

PRACTICE EIGHTY-TWO

As stated at the commencement of the lists of Prefixes[10] and Suffixes or word-endings, these abbreviations should be thoroughly[20] memorized by reading and copying. Their usefulness is immediately obvious,[30] and it seems almost unnecessary to stress the fundamental desirability[40] of a complete knowledge of their application. The majority of[50] these syllables occur with considerable frequency, and such outlines as[60] *possibility, majority, psychological, self-control,* are very compact, compared with the[70] outlines which would result if the forms were written out[80] fully.

Therefore, you are advised to copy out all the[90] examples given, avoiding carelessness in outline formation, and particularly paying[100] proper attention to detail. To be able to write shorthand[110] with skill and efficiency is an accomplishment of much usefulness,[120] and time spent now in accomplishing your object is time[130] extremely well spent.   (133 words)

PRACTICE EIGHTY-THREE

In a mood of introspection I looked backward and I[10] looked forward. As I was even then a fairly old[20] man I had a longer span to contemplate when peering[30] into the past than when searching forward. I deserved the[40] description of a self-made man, and I had every justification[50] for a certain feeling of pride as I thought of[60] all that I had accomplished, of what I hoped had[70] been my intelligent and instructive handling of my life. Hardship[80] I had known, but never hopelessness, and I had had[90] the great happiness of knowing friendship in its highest manifestations.[100] There had been no uniformity about my life, and times[110] of hardship and adversity had been sandwiched between periods of[120] prosperity. I had known irresponsible moments, as well as solemn[130] and responsible occasions; I had been given many an expensive[140] demonstration of the folly of permitting expenditure to outrun income,[150] but throughout it all real sorrow had been unknown to[160] me. As my thoughts turned from the past to the[170] future a sensation of great joyfulness and hopefulness surged through[180] me. Old as I was, I believed that new experiences,[190] new friendships, new possibilities awaited my coming.

(197 words)

Dictation Test Twelve

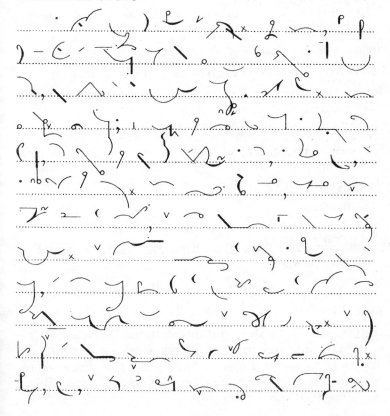

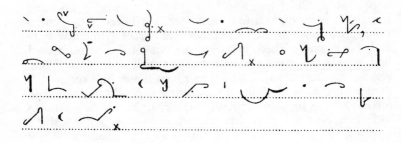

To continue your study of shorthand we recommend you to obtain:

Pitman New Era Shorthand Pocket Dictionary (Pitman)

A New Review of Pitman Shorthand, Coombs (Pitman)

Guide to Phrasing in Pitman New Era Shorthand, Swann (Pitman)

New Phonographic Phrasebook, E. D. Smith (Pitman)

Pitman Shorthand Speedbuilder, New Era edition, Coombs (Pitman)

Pitman Shorthand Speed Development No. 3, New Era edition (Pitman)

Things Fall Apart, Chinua Achebe (Pitman)

Pitman's Shorthand Speed Examinaton Practice No. 1, New Era edition (Pitman)

That There Dog of Mine, New Era edition (Pitman)

Cassettes:

Pre-recorded Cassettes containing timed dictation of all the material appearing in *Pitman Shorthand Speed Development No. 3* and *Pitman's Shorthand Speed Examination Practice No. 1* are available from Cashpost Service, Book Centre, Southport PR9 9YF.

SPECIAL OUTLINES

The shorthand writer is advised to memorize the following pairs of outlines for words which have the same consonantal structure and which, if not distinguished, might cause misreading.

ABANDONED		ABUNDANT	
AGENT		GENTLEMAN	
ALCOHOL		ALKALI	
AVAILABLE		VALUABLE	
BEAUTIFUL		PITIFUL	
BURIAL		BIRTH	
CAUSED		COST	
CONSIDERATE		CONSIDERED	
DEAREST		TRUEST	
DEFER		DIFFER	
DIVERSE		ADVERSE	
EARNESTLY		ERRONEOUSLY	
ELABORATE		LABOURED	
EVENTUALLY		EVIDENTLY	
FAVOURITE		FAVOURED	
FORGET		FORGIVE	
FUTILE		FATAL	

163

GRADUALLY		GREATLY	
GUIDANCE		GOODNESS	
HARDIEST		HARDEST	
HEARTILY		HARDLY	
HEARTY		HARDY	
INEVITABLE		UNAVOIDABLE	
INGOT		NUGGET	
Mrs.		MISSES	
NEEDLESS		ENDLESS	
NEWEST		NEXT	
NOTABLE		NOBLE	
PARTICULARLY		BROADLY	
PERSECUTE		PROSECUTE	
POOR		PURE	
POOREST		PUREST	
PREFER		PROFFER	
QUEER		CLEAR	
SACRED		SECRET	
SITUATION		STATION	
UNDEFINED		INDEFINITE	
UNSOILED		UNSOLD	

SHORT FORMS
Arranged alphabetically

A

a	
accord-ing	
advantage	
advertise- -ment-d	
all	
altogether	
an	
and	
any	
anything	
are	
as	

B

balance	
balanced	
be	
because	
become	
been	

belief	
believe-d	
beyond	
build-ing	
but	

C

call	
can	
cannot	
care	
chair	
character	
cheer	
child	
circumstance	
cold	
come	
could	

D

danger	
dear	

deliver-y-ed		**G**	
description		general-ly	
different-ce		gentleman	
difficult		gentlemen	
difficulty		give-n	
do		go	
doctor, Dr.		gold	
during		govern-ed	
		government	
E		great	
English		guard	
equal-ly			
equalled		**H**	
especial-ly		had	
everything		hand	
exchange-d		has	
expect-ed		have	
eye		he	
		him	
F		himself	
February		his	
financial-ly		hour	
first		how	
for		however	
from			

I

I	∨
immediate	
important-ce	
impossible	
improve-d- -ment	
in	
income	
inconvenience- -t-ly	
influence	
influenced	
inform-ed	
information	
inspect-ed-ion	
instruction	
instructive	
insurance	
interest	
investigation	
is	
it	
itself	

J

January	

K

knowledge	

L

language	
large	
largely	
larger	
largest	
liberty	

M

me	
member	
mere	
more	
most	
Mr.	
much	
myself	

N

near	
never	

nevertheless		**P**	
next		particular	
nor		people	
northern		pleasure	
nothing		practic(s)e-d	
November		principal-ly	
number-ed		principle	
		probable-ly-ility	
O		public	
object-ed		publication	
objection		publish-ed	
of		put	
on		**Q**	
opinion		quite	
opportunity		**R**	
organization		rather	
organize-d		regular	
ought		remark-ed	
our		remember-ed	
ourselves		represent-ed	
over		representative	
owe		respect-ed	
owing		respectful-ly	
own		responsible-ility	
owner			

169

S

		the	
satisfaction		their	
satisfactory		them	
school		themselves	
schooled		there	
sent		therefore	
several		thing	
shall		think	
short		third	
should		this	
something		those	
southern		though	
speak		thus	
special-ly		till	
subject-ed		to	
sufficient-ly-cy		to be	
sure		together	
surprise		told	
surprised		too	
		toward	
		trade	

T

		tried	
tell		truth	
thank-ed		two	
that			

U

under	‿
usual-ly	⌡

V

very	⌐

W

was	)
we	⟋
what	⊃
whatever	⊇
when	⊂
whenever	⊊
whether	⟋
which	∕
who	∕
whose	)

why	∟
wish	⌡
wished	⌡
with	⟨
within	⟨
without	⟨
wonderful-ly	⟋
word	⌐
would	⊃
writer	⟋

Y

yard	⌐
year	⌐
you	∩
young	‿
your	⌐
yesterday	↗

ADDITIONAL CONTRACTIONS

LIST ONE

The following additional contractions will be found useful in high-speed writing.

A

acknowledge

administration

administrative

administrator

appointment

arbitrary

arbitration

architect-ure-al

assignment

B

bankruptcy

behalf

C

capable

certificate

chaired

characteristic

cheered

contentment

D

defective

deficient-ly-cy

deliverance

democracy-atic

demonstrate

demonstration

destruction

discharge-d

distinguish-ed

E

efficient-ly-cy

electric

electrical

electricity

emergency

England

enlarge

enlargement

entertainment

enthusiastic-m

establish-ed- -ment		**L**	
executive		legislative	
executor		legislature	
expediency		**M**	
expenditure		manufacture-d	
expensive		manufacturer	
F		manuscript	
familiar-ity		mathematics	
I		maximum	
identical		mechanical-ly	
identification		messenger	
imperfect-ion-ly		minimum	
incorporated		ministry	
independent- -ly-ce		misfortune	
indispensable-ly		monstrous	
individual-ly		mortgage-d	
influential-ly		**N**	
intelligence		neglect-ed	
intelligent-ly		negligence	
introduction		notwithstanding	
investment		**O**	
irregular		objectionable	
J		objective	
jurisdiction		**P**	
justification		passenger	
		peculiar-ity	

perform-ed	
performance	
practicable	
prejudice-d--ial-ly	
preliminary	
production	
productive	
project-ed	
proportion-ed	
prospective	
publisher	
Q	
questionable-ly	
R	
reform-ed	
remarkable-ly	
representation	
republic	
republican	
respective	
respectively	
S	
selfish-ness	
sensible-ly--ility	

significance	
significant / signify-ied	
spirit	
stranger	
subscribe-d	
subscription	
substantial-ly	
suspect-ed	
sympathetic	
T	
telegram	
telegraphic	
thankful	
U	
unanimous-ly	
uniform-ity-ly	
universal	
universe	
university	
V	
valuation	
W	
welcome	

LIST TWO

A

abandonment

administrate

administratrix

amalgamate

amalgamation

arbitrate

arbitrator

attainment

C

circumstantial

contingency

cross-examina-
tion

cross-examine-d

D

denomination-al

destructive

destructively

E

enlarger

enlightenment

executrix

exigency

extinguish-ed

F

falsification

familiarization

familiarize

G

generalization

H

henceforward

howsoever

I

imperturbable

inconsiderate

informer

inscribe-d

intelligible-ly

irrecoverable-
-ly

irremovable-ly

irrespective

irresponsible-
-ility

M

magnetic-ism

mathematical-
-ly

mathematician

metropolitan

O

obstruction

obstructive

oneself

organizer

P

performer

perpendicular

perspective

proficient-ly-cy

proportionate-
-ly

prospectus

R

recoverable

reformer

relinquish-ed

remonstrance

remonstrate

removable

reproduction

retrospect

retrospection

retrospective

S

signification

stringency

subjection

subjective

T

thenceforward

U

unanimity

universality

unprincipled

W

whensoever

whereinsoever

wheresoever

whithersoever

READING PRACTICE

A SCHOOLBOY'S RUSE

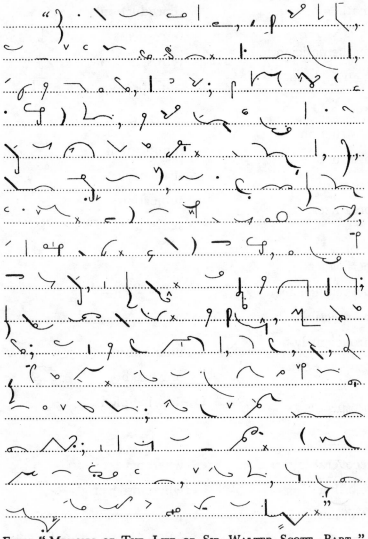

FROM "MEMOIRS OF THE LIFE OF SIR WALTER SCOTT, BART.,"
BY J. G. LOCKHART

AUTUMN SUNSET

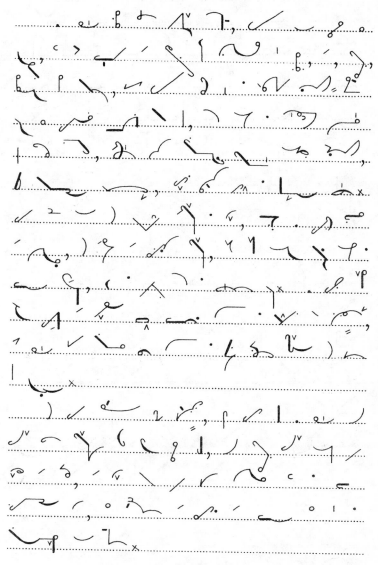

FROM "ESSAYS," BY HENRY DAVID THOREAU

178

FRIENDSHIP

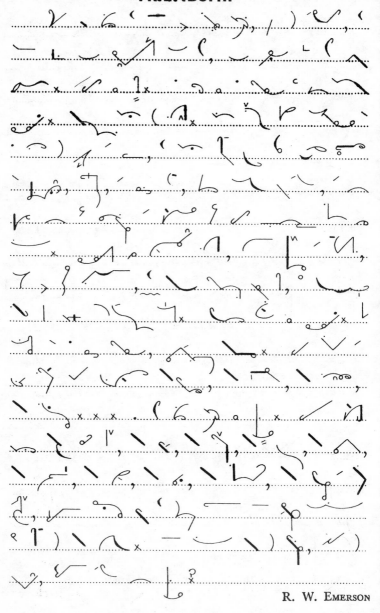

R. W. EMERSON

WHEN POET MEETS POET

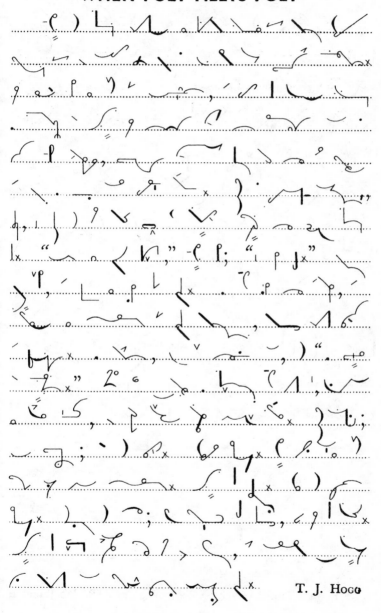

T. J. Hogg

A DOG'S LIFE

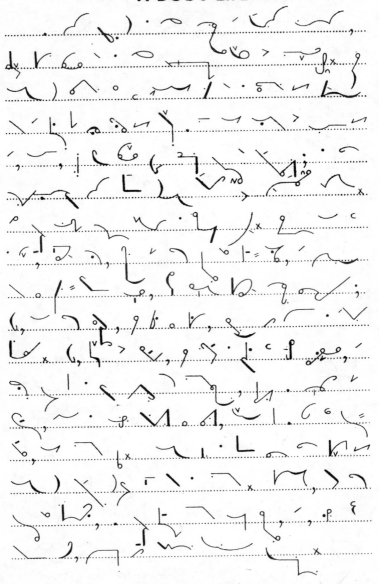

FROM "THE STORY OF A FEATHER," BY DOUGLAS JERROLD

FOR SERVICES RENDERED!

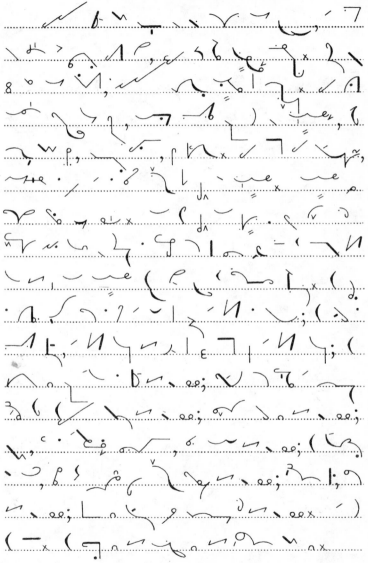

FROM "INNOCENTS ABROAD," BY MARK TWAIN

PARIS AT DAYBREAK

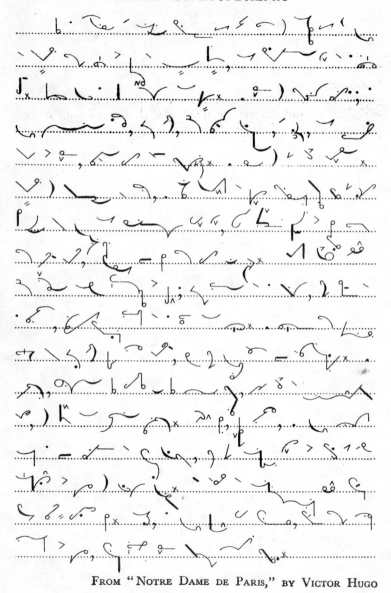

FROM "Notre Dame de Paris," by Victor Hugo